Detachment is a _____ _____ _____ gripping authority rooted in his real-life experience—a journey to bonding love, light, and life. He combines a taut narrative with an inside look at spiritual formation as a way of life. Powerful and timely.

Dr. Wess Pinkham
V.P. of Academics, Dean
Shiloh University

Dr. Colson with his visionary insight has provided a valuable resource for the kingdom of God that will be helpful for personal and corporate development for years to come.

Dr. B. Darrell Bewley
Ministries Coordinator
Tennessee Church of God State Office

As I read the table of contents the excitement was overwhelming and increased as I read each chapter title. I knew God had given Dr. Colson a powerful revelation on how our divine DNA can be unlocked. Tony reveals keys that will help you discover your potential and achieve greatness. After observing the Colson family, I can say that Tony and his wife, LaShea, have been successful implementing these principles within their own home. You are next. You don't have to stay locked up another day!

Pastor Denise Boggs
Author, Teacher, Co-Founder of Living Waters Ministry

Betty,
Thank you so much for your support through the years. We love you. May this book help you achieve your greatest potential!
Tony

UNLOCKING YOUR DIVINE DNA

Escaping Your Past, Embracing Your Identity, and Entering Your Future

Tony Colson — 2 Cor. 3:18

DR. TONY COLSON

AUTHOR ACADEMY elite

Copyright © 2017 Tony L. Colson

All rights reserved. No part of this book may be reproduced without written permission from the author, except in the case of reprints in the context of reviews.

Unless otherwise indicated, Scripture quotations are from the ESV® Bible (The Holy Bible, English Standard Version®), copyright © 2001 by Crossway, a publishing ministry of Good News Publishers. Used by permission. All rights reserved."

Other Bibles Used As Marked:

Scripture quotations marked HCSB®, are taken from the Holman Christian Standard Bible®, Copyright © 1999, 2000, 2002, 2003, 2009 by Holman Bible Publishers. Used by permission. HCSB® is a federally registered trademark of Holman Bible Publishers.

Scripture quotations taken from the New American Standard Bible® (NASB), Copyright © 1960, 1962, 1963, 1968, 1971, 1972, 1973, 1975, 1977, 1995 by The Lockman Foundation. Used by permission. www.Lockman.org

Scripture quotations marked (NIV) are taken from the Holy Bible, New International Version®, NIV®. Copyright © 1973, 1978, 1984, 2011 by Biblica, Inc.™ Used by permission of Zondervan. All rights reserved worldwide. www.zondervan.com The "NIV" and "New International Version" are trademarks registered in the United States Patent and Trademark Office by Biblica, Inc.™

Scripture quotations marked (NKJV) are taken from the New King James Version, © 1979, 1980, 1982 by Thomas Nelson, Inc. Used by permission. All rights reserved.

Library of Congress Control Number: 2017904737
Author Academy Elite, Powell, OH

Paperback: 978-1-946114-54-9
Hardback: 978-1-946114-55-6

Printed in the United States of America

Dedication

I would never have finished this book without the encouragement of my wife. We have explored the world together for more than twenty years. She has stood by me, she has pushed me, and, when necessary, she has pulled me back. Thank you, LaShea, for ALWAYS believing in me—even when I didn't believe in myself. God blessed me with a wonderful, beautiful gift in you. I love you.

To my children: Kiera, Makena, Aliyah, and Tegan—I love you! Thanks for letting daddy work during those times I couldn't be with you. You have been so patient with the process. You gave me the opportunity to pursue my dream and now I encourage you to pursue your dreams with all your heart. Nothing is impossible if you believe (and if you work real hard)!

Lastly, to my moms! I am so thankful for your love for me. Mom (Aleene Brooks) and Momma Grace (Grace Loudin)–you both are beautiful women of God. I am indebted to God that He chose you to be in my life. Any rewards that I have in heaven should be credited to your accounts as well. You have reflected God's image with excellence!

I love my family!

CONTENTS

Foreword by Pastor Ron Carpenter, Jr. ix
Acknowledgments xi
Introduction: A Small Lie xiii

PART ONE
ESCAPING YOUR PAST

1   Original Intent 3
     The Problem Isn't Your Humanity

2   Created For Glory 9
     According To His Kind

3   The Fall... 18
     What Happened IN You

4   The Fallout... 35
     What Happened TO You

5   The Fall Guy....................................... 44
     What Happened FOR You

PART TWO
EMBRACING YOUR IDENTITY

6   Your Divine DNA: Blessing 51
     The Source Of Glory

7   Your Divine DNA: Increase 62
     The Expectation of Glory

8   Your Divine DNA: Dominion 80
The Position of Glory

9   Your Divine DNA: Healthy Relationships 86
The Dance of Glory

10 Your Divine DNA: Purpose 99
The Work of Glory

PART THREE
ENTERING YOUR FUTURE

11 The Divine Transfer 121
On Earth As It Is In Heaven

12 The Mirror Mindset 131
Don't Forget Who You Really Are

13 The Take Method 140
A Strategy For Building Healthy Relationships

14 Principles, Priorities, and Pursuits 151
A Practical Guide To Achieving Your Potential

Epilogue: A Vision Of Glory:
*What If Everyone Unlocked
Their Divine DNA?* 167

Endnotes 173

About The Author 177

FOREWORD
RON CARPENTER, JR.

There is so much more in you. You are a masterpiece designed by God Himself. Oftentimes, we underestimate who God created us to be. I dedicate my life to helping people understand the message of the Kingdom. To me, there is a lot more to being a Christian then going to church and one day going to heaven. God intends for heaven to come to you now!

In Psalm 8:5, there is something special about humanity. God made us capable of greatness on the earth. The Psalmist says that you and I were created a "little lower" than God Himself. There is so much potential within you but without a revelation you will never see it. Tony Colson, one of my spiritual sons, has written this book to empower you with the keys that will unlock the potential of the Kingdom in your life. Tony has uncovered a powerful reality about who you are. You are designed for glory. In Part Two: Embracing

Your Identity, he will help you discover the five components of your Divine DNA. You are going to be excited to know that you have been empowered with blessing, equipped to increase, positioned to rule, created for healthy relationships and called to a unique purpose! You have a divine DNA waiting to be released to the world. Your divine DNA is so valuable that Jesus Himself came to give it back to you.

Humbly, Tony shares his personal struggle which involved disappointment, confusion, and fear. God transformed him and He will transform you. Tony will guide you to the place of escaping your past, embracing your identity, and entering your future. This is not a theological book with good theories. He has included practical instructions and keys that will work in your life. You will be encouraged as you realize just how much potential you have. You don't have to wait one more minute to activate the power of God in your life. It's time that you finally embraced everything that God has for you. It's time for you to unlock your divine DNA!

Pastor Ron Carpenter, Jr.
Senior Pastor
Redemption Church
myredemption.cc

ACKNOWLEDGMENTS

I would like to acknowledge the impact that Dr. Darrell Bewley has made on my life and marriage. Without his faithful support and wise counsel, I would not be at this place in my life. Thank you for standing for and with us. You are a major reason I made it!

I would like to honor Pastors Ron and Hope Carpenter, Jr. for the role they have served in my life and family. Your lives and the ministries of Redemption Church have been a significant part of my healing. My wife and family are healthier today because of your faithful service and your undying commitment to Christ. Thank you!

Special thanks to Melody Scott and Tamela Jett for editing and correcting things I wouldn't have noticed. I appreciate you both.

Lastly, I would like to acknowledge my dependence upon Jesus. You are my Rock, my Savior! I am still alive and in ministry because you finish what you start. You amaze me with your faithfulness. Thank you for giving me the opportunity to live life to the full!

INTRODUCTION
A SMALL LIE

> "For as he thinks within himself, so he is."
> —King Solomon (Proverbs 23:7 NASB)

On a cloudy fall day, Jim puts his folding chair and cooler in the back seat of his car. It is an early Saturday morning with that brisk "It's football time!" feeling in the air. He gets into the driver's seat, adjusts his seat forward, and starts the engine. Jim backs out of his driveway and makes his way to the local ballfield, where scores of young boys would be going head to head while experiencing the game of football throughout the day. Jim loved to watch the boys play. Yet Jim wasn't there to watch a son or a nephew or even a friend's son. He was there because he had a dream. He longed to have a son of his own. Yet the doctors had told him and his wife that it was impossible for them to have another child.

The events suggested above would have been a similar scenario to multiple Saturdays when Jim would vicariously live out his desire to be a dad through a view from the stands. But a "no" from the doctor seemed to suggest this reality would never happen. After coming to the conclusion that their longing for a son wouldn't happen the natural way, Jim and Aleene decided to adopt. They had already been serving as foster parents, so they were somewhat familiar with the process. They made the necessary phone calls and began their wait.

It was at this point of surrender—and yet determination—that Aleene "surprisingly" became pregnant. What the doctors had said would be impossible was now a small child forming within her womb. Anticipation grew as the days and weeks passed. Finally, the day came, and it was confirmed—Jim was having a boy!

Jim and Aleene named him Tony. Tony Lyn Colson.

I was born on August 14, 1971. I wish I could say we lived happily ever after, but life isn't always fair. Eight years later, my daddy was diagnosed with lymphoma and died. Not long after my dad's death, I never played football again. My mom just couldn't bear my participation in football—just too many scary moments for her. Nevertheless, life wasn't over for us, although life was different. The pain caused by the loss of such a great man was unbearable, but my mom tried to bury it and move forward with her life. After that, affection and endearing words were not expressed as often in our day-to-day interactions. Life was different. Scarred by this tragedy of life and faith, she loved us the best way she knew how. She raised me and my two siblings as a single mother for a few years and then remarried.

Honorably, my father wanted her to find a man who could replace him. Unfortunately, the person who won my mom's heart had hidden a dark side that would be discovered shortly after their wedding day. In private, he was different from the nice, hardworking man with whom she had fallen in love. Behind closed doors, he was a tyrant and cultivated an atmosphere of continual hurt and pain for four already broken people.

We became more broken and less alive. The mental and emotional abuse took its toll on each of us. Fear was our new "normal." Joy was absent. The family that my dad longed for was lost within the storm of a dysfunctional home. Death had not just stolen my dad; it had stolen our experience of being a family. The words "I love you" fell silent to the crying out from broken hearts just trying to survive.

As the days passed, this little boy began to grow up. But inside, the longing for a dad never ceased. Thankfully, my uncle stepped up and attempted to fulfill a "daddy's" role for me. Unfortunately, right before my wedding day, he was taken from me. A weak and damaged heart finally got the best of him. Now death had stolen my "best man" too.

God was gracious and brought other men into my life to help fill my need for a father, but it was always limited by the fact that I wasn't *really* their son. Each of these men had sons of their own, and understandably, that had to be their priority. These conditional, limited relationships, with the "substitute fathers" in my life, slowly deteriorated my trust in all relationships.

Acceptance and belief in my value as a person also suffered. The older I grew, the more I lost trust in what I knew. The way faith had worked in the past didn't seem to work anymore. The trust I had in people who were supposed to love me slipped away with each disappointment. This atmosphere of mistrust and a questioning of everything I had known also led me to a place of questioning my identity.

Who am I?

What is my purpose?

Why am I here?

After arriving at adulthood and marrying a beautiful woman named LaShea, the assault on my identity increased in its intensity. It was 1994 on a rainy day in Eastern Tennessee. LaShea and I said our marriage vows and left for our honeymoon in Jamaica. After our first week of beginning life together, we returned on a Thursday, re-packed our bags, and then left for Europe on Saturday to participate in a Discipleship Training School (DTS) through Youth With A Mission (YWAM). We were so excited!

On one hand, this adventure has tales of castles, the Swiss Alps, buildings that are centuries old, and cultures that we had only read about in textbooks. The DTS gave us the opportunity to see Europe in a unique way. It was also a romantic way to start life together. In the first six months of our marriage, we visited 11 countries and slept in 22 different places.

But like coins, every story has two sides. Life isn't always fair. On this journey, we were appointed to serve under a leader who mostly taught us how NOT to be a leader. It was a very trying time in my life, mentally and emotionally, as the leader seemed to make me constantly choose between submitting to her leadership or being sensitive to my wife's concerns. I learned how the enemy can strategically twist God's Word and ultimately caused me to believe a lie. How many lies have you believed that are presently impacting your life?

In this predicament of trying to determine whether to stand up to a leader who was mishandling her role and attempting to honor my wife who had been wounded by this very leader, I came across a scripture in Philippians 2. At that time, I was reading out of the New International Version. The scripture read like this:

> *Rather, he made himself nothing by taking the very nature of a servant being made in human likeness. And being found in appearance as a man, he humbled himself by becoming obedient to death—even death on a cross!* (Philippians 2:7–8 NIV)

My mind began to focus on the words "made himself nothing." As I began to reflect more and more on this idea of making myself nothing, it began to influence my idea of "me." If Jesus made Himself nothing, then who was I?

As a result, I chose not to stand up for myself (or my wife) because "I am nothing." What I didn't realize was that the enemy had taken these words, which I saw as the Word of God, and slowly, meticulously had begun to assault my identity. The posture that began with not defending myself because of my "nothingness" led tragically further to the idea that nothingness meant I had no true value. If I had no value, then what kind of contribution could I make in the world? Adding to the assault, the enemy used my "failures" as affirmation of my lack of significance. Then the enemy posed a question: If I would do this sin—then why wouldn't I be capable of doing something even worse? I began to lose all confidence in who I was.

After this assault was fully underway, I found myself in a very dark place. I had no real confidence in relationships and no confidence in myself. It opened the door for me to have thoughts I would have never believed possible.

It is amazing how far the enemy can take you if you simply believe a lie. A small lie is like a small key. The problem is that it unlocks the door to darkness. Thankfully, there is another force more powerful than our enemy. His purpose is to straighten out twisted things and to restore identity as He originally intended. He has a plan to transform your darkness into light, your brokenness into wholeness, and your confusion into clarity. I know this because He did it for me!

This book was born out of my journey to discover who I am. Notice, I didn't say "who I was" but who I am. *Unlocking Your Divine DNA* is a process I can't wait for you to discover. This is my way of saying to you that there is hope.

It is my mission to help you realize your true identity and discover your God-given purpose. I have learned a process of recovering what is lost through a journey of transformation. We live in a broken world, and a broken world makes broken people. I was broken. I still have some broken parts, but the transformation has started.

How about you?

Are you ready to find your true purpose?

Are you ready to embrace your divine DNA?

God made a way for people like you and me to escape our past, embrace our identity, and enter our future.

PART ONE

ESCAPING YOUR PAST

CHAPTER 1
ORIGINAL INTENT
THE PROBLEM ISN'T YOUR HUMANITY

"When I discover who I am, I'll be free."
—Ralph Ellison, *Invisible Man*

Who are you?
What is your purpose?
Why are you here?

Does it really matter if you discover and fulfill your purpose? Each person, at one point or another, has faced questions like these, and sometimes they have haunted us more than they have helped us. How can you unlock your "divine DNA?" How can you find your purpose? Let me explain it like this....

As I prepared to leave for work one morning, I came to the realization that my wife, who had taken my car to work, had also taken her car keys with her, and my set was locked inside her car. So I was stuck with two options. I could either call a locksmith and allow them to grant me access to the vehicle or I could find a way to get into my wife's car, retrieve my set of keys, and make it to work on time! The former meant I would be late for work, so I opted for the latter and went in search of a coat hanger. I fished my way through the sunroof and masterfully opened the door. Success! Off to work I went, having accomplished my goal (and music plays as I drive off into the sunset).

Did I mention every coin has two sides? This day of ingenuity on my part would end badly. In my effort to open the sunroof, *masterfully*, I had damaged the seal (music abruptly stops). A metal hanger is not made to open sunroofs. You know what happened next. As her car was parked outside, with this new hole in the sunroof, the weather changed. Evening clouds formed, and ultimately rain appeared. As each drop of rain fell, so did my chances of making it through this experience! The interior roof of the car was soaked by the rain. A damaged seal and soaked upholstery is not a good combination to win points with your wife. I had to find a way to fix it and fast.

I needed a solution. My mind raced for a quick fix—what can dry up the water quickly? The answer came in the form of a hair dryer. Surely this would redeem my standing with my wife.

The hair dryer and I went to work. Unfortunately, it worked a little too well. The roof did get dry, but the heat burned the felt in the process. My bad day descended to a whole other level. The hair dryer did what it was made to do—blow hot air. The problem was that the hair dryer was supposed to dry hair, not a car's upholstery. Misusing it had caused permanent damage by burning a circle onto the felt.

Realizing and honoring the original intent for an object will help the owner use it properly. For instance, during one of my home projects, I may revert to using a wrench as a hammer. Does it work? Sure…sometimes. But the job could have been done better and more effectively if the correct tool would have been used. At times, my substitute tool ends up broken or damaged in some way.

Other times, things are used wrongly because of ignorance, but even innocence doesn't protect us from the danger of misunderstanding purpose. It reminds me of the story of the lady who, for years, cooked a ham following the pattern of her mom.

Step by step, she prepared the ham just as she had seen her mom do it. After some time, she perfected the process and felt as if she had achieved the same great taste and rich flavor as her mother's ham. She decided to invite her mom over and impress her by preparing the ham just like her. The day came, and her mom arrived. The mom was surprised to smell what seemed to be the aroma of "her ham" in the air.

Impressed, she sat down at the dinner table and waited with anticipation for the meal cooked by her daughter. The daughter, glowing with pride, brought a delightfully prepared ham to the table. She served her mother the ham, baked beans, and sweet corn. Her mom was impressed. Her daughter had mastered the taste, the smell, and even the tenderness of the meat. Yet there was one thing that perplexed the mother. Part of the ham had been cut off.

As the meal continued, this began to bother her, and she finally inquired of her daughter by saying, "I am so proud of you. You have prepared a succulent meal. I could not have done it better. I do have one thing that I don't fully understand. Why is part of the ham missing?" Quickly, her daughter responded by saying, "I watched you prepare hams throughout the years, and one of the things that you always did was cut off the end of the ham. I simply followed your example." "Oh, honey!" the mother exclaimed. "The only reason I did that was because I didn't have a pan large enough for the whole ham!"

This innocent "chef" was throwing away good parts of the ham simply because she misunderstood why her mom had cut off the end. She misunderstood the purpose.

As I mentioned above, tools can also be abused and misused as well—sometimes intentionally and sometimes ignorantly. The problem with both the misuse and the abuse is that the tools can suffer damage and ultimately not be able to be used for their original intention. This is the key in our struggle for OUR true identity. We must learn to understand and honor our purpose. Unless we understand our true purpose, we may accomplish certain things in life, but we will never achieve our greatest potential. And worse yet, we may damage things (or people) along the way. All too often we don't understand our purpose, or because we, or someone else, intentionally abuses us, we fail to see it. Like the substitute tool, we find ourselves broken and unable to fulfill our purpose.

All too often, people go through life simply surviving. Their days are filled with little satisfaction and minimal effectiveness. They are broken and bent, and yet because so many of us live like this, we think it is normal. We have normalized abnormality. This brokenness leads us to a place of dysfunction, and we become comfortable with our malfunction. We have even learned to excuse our sin by saying, "I'm only human"—as if humanness is the reason for brokenness. The problem with this excuse is that the only fix would seem to be becoming something other than human—at best something super-human or, at worst, something less than human.

The problem isn't our humanity but something different. Once a person identifies who they were meant to be and then makes their way back to a place of wholeness, they become capable and ready to function with full potential, full humanity. God's will for man hasn't changed. He created us in His likeness then and now wants us to be restored to that same image.

My goal is to guide you along a process of transformation, restoring you back into the person God originally intended when He determined you would exist. You are not the mere result of chance. You are not the result of an accident. You are the creation of God. Unfortunately, even after a person places their trust in Christ for salvation, oftentimes they continue to live beneath their God-given potential.

Your divine DNA starts to unlock when you understand how and why God made you in the first place. An improper mindset with regard to the way God intended humanity to live will result in a lack of personal wholeness and fulfillment. This confusion, this misunderstanding of mankind's potential and purpose, has resulted in too many people like you and me living below our humanity.

There are four benefits that this book will address about this process of discovery. It will:

1. Unpack the key for you to escape the past and have the opportunity to become who you really are!
2. Reveal the significance of personal identity and the impact that identity has on individual potential and the fulfillment of purpose while giving you permission to embrace this new identity.
3. Provide tools and an understanding that will guide you through this process of transformation and open the door for you to enter your future.
4. Help you in becoming whole and ultimately restore you to who you are created to be—*unlocking your divine DNA*.

Also, I want to connect you with a community of people who are on the same journey. This will create an opportunity for you to have the support and accountability needed to go where you cannot go alone. We need each other!

I look forward to the day when you look in the mirror and realize that you are free—you have unlocked your divine DNA.

CHAPTER 2
CREATED FOR GLORY
ACCORDING TO HIS KIND

"The glory of God is the human person fully alive."

—St. Irenaeus[1]

The first question that we must ask on this journey is "How can we know our true identity?" Our culture has different sayings to encourage people to be true to themselves. You will hear things like "Just be you!" or "Follow your heart." The problem with these mottos is that they are dependent upon the person knowing the truth about themselves. If your heart is confused and you follow it, it will lead you astray. So how can you discover who you really are?

There are two passages in which we can discover what the "image of God" is. The first place in Scripture where the image of God is revealed is literally in "the beginning," or Genesis 1. Read this passage, which describes the creation of the first man and woman.

> Then God said, "Let us make man in our image, after our likeness… (Genesis 1:26a NKJV)

I will spend more time on this later, but I wanted you to see how significant you are. You are an amazing person. You are truly a divine masterpiece. You may not feel like it. Your past may not affirm this kind of idea. Nevertheless, there is something inside that must not be ignored any longer. You are made with a divine DNA. Up until now, it has been locked up, unable to shine. I am getting ready to hand you the keys to unlock your potential!

According to Its Kind

The human body is truly amazing. Here are some facts to ponder:

- Your nose can remember 50,000 different scents.
- The air from a human sneeze can travel at speeds of 100 miles per hour or more. (Maybe when we sneeze, *we* should be telling the people around us "God bless you!" instead of the other way around.)
- There are about 60,000 miles of blood vessels in the human body.
- The human heart pumps about 2,000 gallons of blood through those vessels each and every day.
- The average human head has 100,000 hair follicles. (When I look in the mirror, I don't think I am average).[2]

Whether you believe in God or not, I believe you would agree with me that the human body is pretty phenomenal—incredibly complex and immensely functional. Listening to some people talk about humanity, one would think that we are hopeless, deplorable beings. The Bible, however, has some things to say about humanity that are a lot more glorious than the idea that we are "*only*" human.

When we look at Genesis 1, we find a pattern of God's creation that we should pay attention to, as it relates to God's intention for mankind. Examine the following verses from the creation account:

> *11 Then God said, "Let the earth bring forth grass, the herb that yields seed, and the fruit tree that yields fruit according to its kind, whose seed is in itself, on the earth"; and it was so. 12 And the earth brought forth grass, the herb that yields seed according to its kind, and the tree that yields fruit, whose seed is in itself according to its kind. And God saw that it was good. 21 So God created great sea creatures and every living thing that moves, with which the waters abounded, according to their kind, and every winged bird according to its kind. And God saw that it was good. 24 Then God said, "Let the earth bring forth the living creature according to its kind: cattle and creeping thing and beast of the earth, each according to its kind"; and it was so. 25 And God made the beast of the earth according to its kind, cattle according to its kind, and everything that creeps on the earth according to its kind. And God saw that it was good.* (Genesis 1:11–12, 21, 24–25 NKJV)

Notice in these verses the phrase "according to its kind." This phrase is repeated multiple times as God created herbs, fruit trees, fish in the water, birds of the air, and the animals on the land. It is not a difficult thing to recognize that cattle will reproduce cattle, eagles reproduce eagles, and apples ultimately have the potential to reproduce more apples. God's creative act came with the *intention* that His creation would reproduce after its own kind. Then the next two verses introduce us to His favorite creation:

> *26 Then God said, "Let Us make man in Our image, according to Our likeness; let them have dominion over the fish of the sea, over the birds of the air, and over the cattle, over all the earth and over every creeping thing that creeps on the earth." 27 So God created man in His own image; in the image of God He created him; male and female He created them.* (Genesis 1:26–27 NKJV)

Did you see it? According to its kind…according to its kind…according to its kind…THEN GOD SAID, "Let us make man IN OUR IMAGE, ACCORDING TO OUR LIKENESS." God made trees, herbs, and animals to reproduce after their kind—THEN He made man with a similar intention. He created you according to His kind. God made you and me to be like Him. Man was created to "reflect" God's image in the earth. All of God's creation had a degree of glory, but only one was given the honor (and responsibility) to be created in His likeness.

The Image of God

The second place we see the image of God revealed is in the life of Jesus Christ when He lived on the earth. According to Hebrews, Jesus is the "express image" of

God (1:3 NKJV). The Apostle Paul declares that Jesus is the "image of the invisible God" (Col. 1:15). Finally, we know according to John 1 that Jesus was the Word and the Word was made flesh. The Word of God reveals the Son of God, who reveals the glory of God. His life, His words, His behaviors, and His actions reveal God's glory to us.

The Image Revealed

In order to get a full understanding of the "image of God," the image that we were created to reflect, we must combine what we learn from God's first man, Adam, and God's second man, Jesus Christ. The book of Genesis reveals five components that were present when God created the first human before he sinned and "fell from glory." Significantly, we find all five of these components in the life of Jesus as He lived on the earth.

> *So God created man in His own image; in the image of God He created him; male and female He created them. Then God blessed them, and God said to them, "Be fruitful and multiply; fill the earth and subdue it; have dominion over the fish of the sea, over the birds of the air, and over every living thing that moves on the earth…Then the Lord God took the man and put him in the garden of Eden to tend and keep it.* (Genesis 1:27–28, 2:15 NKJV)

The five components are:

1. Blessing
2. Increase
3. Dominion

4. Healthy Relationships
5. Purpose

I describe these five components as our divine DNA. God has woven these aspects into the fabric of our being. Unfortunately, for most of us, it is largely hidden. Let's take a few moments and briefly examine these five components both as they are expressed in Genesis and in the life of Jesus while He lived on the earth. Remember, Jesus did not come to show us up or to condemn us. Jesus came as "the way"—to show us the way to live. He came as "the life"—to demonstrate the kind of life we were to have. And He came as the "truth"—to set us free to walk in our original intention of glory (See John 14:6). We are not to look at Jesus and excuse ourselves by saying, "Well, you know...He's Jesus, and that's why He is able to do those things." No, we are to say, "That's Jesus, and that's what I have the potential to become!" Let's take a closer look at the divine DNA.

First, we discover the component that empowers mankind to fulfill this intention of glorious living. God **blessed** them. In Ephesians 1:3, we see that we have been blessed with every spiritual blessing in the heavenly places. You have everything you need to fulfill your God-intended purpose to live life to the full.

Next, God says to man,- "Be **fruitful** and multiply." God intends for you to prosper and be fruitful. He intends for you to be productive and to see increase in your life. You were created for glorious increase. In the book of Luke, we see that even Jesus "increased in wisdom and stature, and in favor with God and men" (Luke 2:52 NKJV).

Then, God says, "Have **dominion**." It is God's divine intention that you rule in life and have dominion. We are called to be "more than conquerors" (Romans 8:37). Jesus demonstrated this power to rule as He spoke to the wind and waves and said, "Peace, be still," and they obeyed (Mark 4:39). Immediately after calming the storm on the sea, He took authority over an "internal storm" in a man on the other side of the shore. (See Mark 5:1-15) God's intention is for us is to rule over the storms around us and the storms within us.

Fourthly, being created in His image suggests that we were created to have **healthy relationships**. God declares that man was to be created in *"their"* image—male and female He created us. When we reflect on the relationship among the Trinity, we realize that God was in perfect unity with Himself. The three persons of the Godhead never argue, are never in competition, and never hurt or deceive each other. They function by being complementary, and each one is a part of the whole. Remember, the Father said, "…This is My beloved Son, in whom I am well pleased" (Matthew 3:17 NKJV). Then Jesus talks about His Father as the one to whom He submits. Finally, the Holy Spirit is seen as the one who works in perfect harmony with the others as our teacher. God intends that man have glorious relationships that express unity, oneness, and fulfillment.

Lastly, as you begin to see who you are—when you realize the wonder of your created being—you learn the key that will unlock your divine DNA as you understand that your existence on Earth is meant for so much more than just passing time. Grasping the significance of being resourced with God's blessing, able to increase, positioned to rule, and connected to others through healthy relationships, you will see that there is something much greater at work. God has assigned you a unique and specific **purpose**, and this purpose is directly related to your becoming a reflection of Him. God has created you to be like Him on the earth. Your purpose is to order the earthly realm to reflect the heavenly realm. As more and more individuals begin to unlock their divine DNA and truly start to reflect God, the earth will start looking like heaven.

Each of these components complement and rely on the others. They cannot be separated. When these five components are properly at work in us, we are on the journey of transformation—a journey to increasing glory. We begin to operate as God originally intended mankind to function. Again, He created *you* to reflect Him in the earth. You were created with a purpose, and you have been given everything you need to achieve it.

In summary, we see that God's original creation was blessed and meant to be fruitful, to have dominion, to have healthy relationships, and ultimately to serve a purpose that brings glory to God. As we look back to this original creation, we also find our intended purpose from God. Jesus Christ came to renew this image in us. He came to transform us from sin to glory and then from glory to more glory!

> *But we all, with unveiled face, beholding as in a mirror the glory of the Lord, are being transformed into the same image from glory to glory, just as by the Spirit of the Lord.* (2 Corinthians 3:18 NKJV)

This book is going to take you on a journey of transformation—a journey to transform you from who you are now to becoming who you really are as God has already intended. My commitment to you is to be your tour guide along the journey.

The commitment I am asking from you is to lay aside your old driver's manual. When you get a new car, you don't use your old car's manual. Your new car works differently. Your new car has different features. Look at this book as a new manual based on your divine DNA. Take a moment to make these five declarations with me:

I am blessed.
I am fruitful.
I am victorious.
I have healthy relationships.
I am fulfilled in purpose.

Now let's go unlock your divine DNA. Let's start by escaping the past.

CHAPTER 3
THE FALL
WHAT HAPPENED IN YOU

"What you might see as depravity is, to me, just another aspect of the human condition."

—Asia Argento[3]

So what happened? If humanity was created with such glory and potential, why is the world in such bad shape? The current state of our world couldn't be the intention of God, could it? The world as it is today can be traced back to the original man and woman—the same two persons who were created in the image of God and in His glory. You know them as Adam and Eve. Imagine what it must have been like being the very first created man and woman. Lush gardens, exotic animals, tropical

THE FALL   19

birds, mountains, and refreshing rivers. It was *literally* paradise. One might even say heaven on Earth.

This man and woman delighted in the fullness of life. There was no hatred, fear, shame, divorce, arguments, bankruptcy, hunger, or lack. Humankind existed in total bliss on the earth *as God intended*. The man was placed in the Garden in order to tend and keep it. This task was his responsibility. The man was commissioned with naming everything (See Genesis 2:19,20). Whatever Adam saw, he named it, and that's what it was. It's identity was established by this representative chosen to order earthly life. He was blessed; equipped to increase; positioned to rule; graced with a helpmate to create enjoyable, healthy relationships; and charged with purpose.

God intended life to be nothing less than…well… heaven on Earth. As humanity was placed here to steward the earth, his role was to represent God to the earthly realm. When man showed up, the earth was to see God. This was God's intention. Unfortunately, darkness entered this scene of divine perfection. In Genesis 3, we are introduced to an infamous character from the story of creation. This character would initiate a change in human existence that can still be felt today.

Let me introduce him by quoting directly from the Bible: "Now the serpent was more crafty than any other beast of the field that the Lord God had made" (Genesis 3:1). It's as if the author is drawing our attention to the slyness of this important character. The first two chapters had introduced us to the magnificence of a God who can speak and create out of nothing. Our imaginations are stimulated beyond capacity as we imagine mountains being formed, mists coming up from the ground, and the positioning of the moon and the sun into places of authority. Our breath is taken away as we reflect on the reality that God breathed life into man and the incredible moment when God, who spoke everything into existence, stoops down and begins to masterfully shape the first man out of the dust of the earth. God was an artist making His best masterpiece. This creature was different. This one was personal. This one was like Himself.

Without warning, the author transitions by saying, "Now the serpent was more crafty than any other beast that God had made." Regardless of whether or not you believe the serpent was literally the devil or merely possessed by the devil, it is obvious that he is the representation of evil to the earth in the same way man represented God to the earth. The serpent came to pick a fight with Eve. Unfortunately, Eve didn't recognize this creature as an enemy. He was not just an enemy to Eve though; he was an enemy to all of creation and to God as well. This is the trick that all of us should prepare ourselves to recognize.

The battles for destiny always involve more than just us! Whether we win or lose, the impact is felt for generations. This is why I want you to embrace your true identity. I want you to take back what the enemy stole from you. I want you to reclaim the ground that our ancestors shamefully surrendered. I want you to pay intention to the process the serpent masterfully executed against God's image in the earth. The serpent was the most crafty beast. Humanity was not a beast. Nevertheless, the Fall reduced man and woman to something less than God intended. Let's go deeper into the story....

One Rule, One Tree

Adam and Eve had one rule.

What a simple life, huh? Don't do this one thing and everything else will be fine. They could enjoy all the pleasures of life in the garden—every delight, wonderful taste, and exhilarating scent. God placed everything in their hands. Adam was simply commissioned to tend and keep the garden. The only command was for the couple NOT to eat the fruit from one tree. This tree is the center of our story, and it becomes the point where the first man takes a dreadful turn.

Following the brief but chilling introduction of the serpent, the writer opens the scene by simply saying, "The serpent said to the woman." Remember that the world was much different than the world in which we live. It is plausible that the animals and humans communicated in a way that is foreign to us. The writer of Genesis didn't feel obligated to explain why or how the serpent spoke. He just starts the narrative with stating that he spoke. Interestingly, the serpent begins with a question. He asks the woman, **"Did God really say** you can't eat of every tree in the Garden?" This cunning approach began with a light touch that disguised the weighty consequence of staying engaged in the conversation.

I am almost certain that the tone in which the serpent asked this question was not harsh or accusatory either. It was probably of a gentle, inquisitive tone that appealed to the innocence of Earth's first woman. He knew he wouldn't be received by challenging God at this point in the relationship, so he began by questioning His Word. This, of course, is the first step in questioning one's character. Once we lose trust in a person's word, we have much less confidence in who they are. The serpent recognized he couldn't incite disobedience until he had generated a sense of distrust. His strategy was not to push her overboard but rather cause her to trip over her own missteps.

The strategic questioning of the woman got her talking. This was the first step to destruction—the exchange of words centered around a question. Let me remind you that the world in which you and I live was the product of "words." Words have the power to create and to destroy. Words are like a weapon. When used properly, they can guard and provide protection. On the other hand, words from the mouth of an enemy can devastate the strongest of souls. A dialogue with the enemy opens the door to hell itself.

> **The enemy's strategy is not to push us overboard but rather to cause us to trip over our own missteps.**

Death and life are in the power of the tongue…(Proverbs 18:21 NKJV)

No More Games

Taking advantage of her innocence, the serpent ups the ante and declares without apology, "You will not surely die!" The serpent has now turned combative. He has moved past testing Eve. The sly one now accuses God. Eve's willingness to join in the conversation opens the door for the enemy's advance. He says that God has not been open and honest with her about everything. It is clear that Eve isn't ready for his response because she has no answer for his bold challenge.

I want you to be ready to answer your enemy. I want you to have the power to overcome the subtle schemes or bold attacks of your foe so that you can walk out your God-given purpose. In order to embrace your identity, you have to first escape your past, which profoundly impacts how you are living today. If you are not careful, the past will also dictate who you are becoming. Your experiences, your authority figures, and the interpretations of your feelings have impacted your personal identity today. These past experiences inform, and even more significantly, they script out your daily responses. Realizing what happened in Genesis 3 will assist you in understanding who you are and who you are meant to be.

Adam and Eve were placed on the earth as God's image. Adam was a patriarchal representative for all mankind. The Bible teaches us the significant difference between Eve's response to the serpent and the way Adam responded. Eve partook of the fruit because she was deceived. The serpent pulled one over on her. Adversely, the Bible never says Adam was deceived. Being influenced by Eve, he chose willingly and knowingly to disregard the command of God. Perhaps Adam was attempting to please his wife and be accepted by her. He disregarded God's instruction because of her promptings. This intentional disobedience led to a terrible tragedy. We will talk about the significance of roles in our relationships in a later chapter, but understand that God is a God of order. Paul declared that everything "should be done decently and in order" (1 Cor. 14:40). Is your life in order? Are you honoring the principles that God has put in place to order your life? If not, you are likely frustrated and unfulfilled. It is time to use the keys of the Kingdom to lock up the past and unlock your future!

The serpent vandalized God's beautiful work of art. He came to usurp control and to take away from Adam and Eve what was rightfully theirs. In order to do this, he used a strategy that is still in operation today. As you recognize this tactic, you will learn to protect your divine DNA from the lies of your enemy. The enemy has a three-pronged attack that he uses to enslave humanity, and his goal is to diminish humanity's glory. A mirror with scratches and scars on its surface cannot properly reflect images. Thus, the scar of sin so damaged humanity that we could not reflect the true image of God. In other words, we fell short of glory.

> *for all have sinned and fall short of the glory of God…* (Romans 3:23 NKJV)

How does the enemy lead us into sinful actions and patterns? He has a well-thought-out plan, and each of us are in his gun sights. Don't fail to recognize this attack since recognizing it could save your future!

The Three-Pronged Attack of the Enemy:

1. He questions God's Word.
2. He questions our identity.
3. He questions the consequences of our disobedience.

Did He Really Say That?

First, the enemy questions God's Word in order to establish a challenge to His character. As long we trust God, we will obey God. When you take Him at His Word, you will follow His Word without fail. The adversary knows obedience and disobedience are heart issues. If he can get us to question God's Word, we will begin to question whether or not God is trustworthy. We will wonder whether He is who He says He is. Is He really concerned about us? Perhaps we might even question whether or not what He says is in our best interests. The serpent says to the woman, "God knows when you eat of it you are going to be like Him." This subtle assertion suggests that God is afraid of what man can become. The accuser implies that God is threatened by humanity's potential. (In actuality, he is the one threatened by humanity's potential.) The crafty one suggests that God is just trying to keep you from being as good as Him; God is keeping a secret from you in order to hold you back. There is more for you to experience, and you have the right to enjoy it. These questions are meant to open your heart to options—his options.

Our enemy works the same way today. He places doubts in our minds about the Bible—God's Word. We begin to question its relevance, whether or not the Bible really has our best interests in mind. Besides, we say to ourselves, it is thousands of years old. It is the product of an entirely different age. How can it relate to our world of technology, our post-modern thinking, and our age of tolerance? This leads to our questioning of God's character. Once we have begun the descent into questioning His Word, we begin to question who He is. Then we have opened the door to a world we were never meant to know.

What You See Is What You Get

The second challenge relates to identity. The attack is not just focused on us questioning who God is. The enemy takes advantage of the open door and subtly attacks us as well. If God is not who He says He is, perhaps we are not who we thought we were. Personal identity is the way we interpret our personhood. If the enemy can get us to question who we are, he can influence what we do, and behavior is an expression of identity. The serpent cunningly says to the woman, "God knows that when you eat of the fruit you will actually be like Him, knowing good and evil." This was a two-faced statement. One side was a lie. The other side was true. As they say, "perception is reality."

As a man thinks in his heart, so is he. (Proverbs 23:7 NKJV)

Let me remind you that Adam and Eve were <u>already like</u> God. His creative work in the beginning was to fashion us in His "likeness." Eve was already created in God's likeness, and yet the enemy sowed a seed of deception into her thinking. When she believed the lie, a whole new world became possible. He was trying to convince her that there was something different, something *more* she was supposed to be. This confusion of identity opened her up to experiencing life in a way God never intended. His prized possession was never supposed to lose. The serpent disputed her identity in order to get her to live life contrary to her true personhood.

The enemy does the same to you and me. His strategy is to cause us to question our identity so that we will embrace a wrong interpretation of our personhood.

If we see ourselves differently than the way God created us, then we will live life contrary to the way God intended. In essence, Eve had everything she needed and was everything she needed to be. The serpent tricked her by causing her to think something wasn't complete. More accurately, he conned her into believing *she* wasn't complete. The enemy works in our minds, attempting to skew our perspective. If he can change our view of ourselves, we will live differently than our intended purpose.

This tactic creates the opportunity for you and me to choose things that seem right and feel right but, ultimately, are disastrously wrong for us. We get into relationships, choose careers, take substances, and cling to patterns that are harmful to us. And then we justify it by saying, "It's just the way I am," or "I am being true to myself." Some of us take the victim approach and blame others for our failures. Either way, we miss the mark. This skillful method causes people to settle for a life that is far less than what God intended.

The truth of the serpent's statement must also be examined. He said to her, "You will be like God, knowing good and evil." A good liar always uses a little truth to sell the lie. The true part of the statement was that they would "know good and evil." Up to this point, Adam and Eve didn't know good *and* evil. The Earth's first couple only knew good. They experienced total good.

Good health.
Good weather.
Good food.
Good relationship.
Good God.

This was God's original intention for mankind, and this commandment was meant to guard His original intention for humanity. God's commandments are always meant to protect the blessings God has for you.[4] The next time you consider disobeying God, look past the moment and see the blessing being threatened. You shouldn't approach obedience with the question "What will I miss out on?" Obedience is locking the door in the face of failure. Rather, you should recognize that your act of obedience will position you to walk in God's full blessing. The command or instruction God is asking you to follow is actually His way of protecting you. A commandment is a fence purposed to protect a domain of glory. When we cross the fence, we leave the land of God's protection and find ourselves in a wilderness of darkness. A wrong perspective will make the "grass look greener on the other side" when, in reality, you are right where you should be.

It's Not That Bad...

The third question deals with consequence. The serpent's goal was to incite distrust for God, to create confusion about identity, and to minimize for the reality of consequence. This formula cultivates the right atmosphere for the enemy to lead us to our destruction. He can get us chasing evil like it's the best thing around. Our passions and pursuits are fueled by a devious force that leads us into loss. What do we lose? Glory.

Romans 3:23 tells us "For all have sinned and fallen short of the glory of God." Maybe you have heard this verse interpreted something like this: "Because of sin, humanity will not get to go to heaven." The loss of glory is not losing the opportunity to go to Heaven. It is the loss of glory that we were intended to walk in on the earth. It's more than you not going to heaven; it's heaven not coming to you HERE on Earth. The consequence was "death" and not just physical. This death happened inside you. Sin happened in you. The Fall set up humanity with a loss of personhood, which led to all the other evils that we were not supposed to know.

Sin leads us to a place of knowing evil, which is more damaging than just knowing about evil. Sin brings evil close to us, inside of us. This is the horrible reality of the Fall—sin happened in us. We died. Before Christ, you and I existed on Earth not as human beings but as human *dyings*. The curse of sin touched us so deeply that even our lives were expressed in ways of death: addiction, bondage, fear, distress, hate, lust, brokenness. Can you name the death that you have lived?

Even though we were physically alive, we were dead. We were dead in our sinfulness. Death happened in every realm—spiritually, emotionally, mentally, physically, and relationally. Life was not life as God intended, because of this reality. Yes, God created us in His image, but sin shattered His reflection. Profoundly, this death touched humanity in all three parts of our created nature. God is one God expressed in three persons, namely, the Father, the Son, and the Holy Spirit. We were each created as one person, namely, a body, a soul, and a spirit. As a result of sin, our bodies and souls are gravely distorted in their creation. Our bodies are slowly decaying to the point where one day death will overtake us. Our souls, which consist of our minds, our wills, and our emotions, have been so damaged that humans are terribly fragile beings.

The final place that was impacted by this death was deep within. Our spirits are dead because of sin. As a result, we live our lives making decisions inordinately influenced by the body and the soul. Our bodies tell us that we are too tired to work out. Our emotions are unstable. Our minds are often overwhelmed, confused, or perplexed because of this disorder in life. Lastly, our will is infected with the disease of sinful desires, which constantly pull us into directions that are contrary to our created purpose. Our spirits are the most affected by sin. They are, in essence, dead to God. God intended for us to be intimately connected to Him through the spirit, but before being born again, the spirit remains separate from God and unable to respond to the promptings of the Heavenly Father. Besides communication, the spirit also possesses capacity. The human spirit is that component that houses the capacity to be like God. A "dead spirit" leaves us operating exclusively from our bodies and souls rather than by the spirit.

In the Garden on that fateful day, several things occurred as a result of Eve's deception and Adam's disobedience. The following five evils were imposed on humanity. These five things were evils humans were never supposed to experience:

1. Their eyes were "opened."
2. Shame entered their hearts.
3. Fear overwhelmed their minds.
4. Excuses justified their actions.
5. Judgments turned their blessing into cursing.

Their Eyes Were "Opened"

First, the Bible says that their eyes were "opened." How terrible it is when you first learn a childhood fantasy is not real like you had supposed. Everything you knew up to that point suddenly changed. Technically, it's not that everything changes but that your perspective on everything changes. The way you look at life, and people, and animals, and all of creation changes. This happens on the inside of you. Perception is reality; therefore perception is everything. When sin entered, perception changed for humanity. The problem with this perception is that it was not fantasy. Perception is significant because perception is the driving force of personal identity. Perception has to do with interpretation. When Adam and Eve's eyes were "opened," they began to see through a different lens. Their perspective was no longer a divine perspective. It was now shaded by sinfulness. Sin always darkens one's ability to see clearly.

Shame On You

Next, shame—one of the evils that Adam and Eve were not meant to know—entered their scene. Shame is a like a dark storm cloud at an outdoor wedding. Shame casts a dark shadow over normally bright days. The shame thrown on them as a result of this moment would soon become a heaviness that they could not shake off. It is an unforgiving connection between our present and our past. Shame empowers our past to cause us to avoid opportunities. Shame is a lingering disqualifier that continually holds us trapped to the past. Shame could be illustrated as a long distance runner carrying around a 50-pound weight expecting to win the race. It hinders one's ability to move freely. Shame adds something to you that you were not meant to carry.

Fear Overwhelmed Their Minds

Another dark enemy that has paralyzed humanity throughout the ages is fear. Fear cripples us from stepping into places that are rightfully ours and causes us to believe things that are not true. Imagine how God must have felt on that first trip back to the Garden after the Fall. He enters into His earthly paradise. He sees the animals and the trees and hears the chirping of the birds. Everything seems normal, but He knows that it isn't.

Something isn't right.

This time His children aren't there to greet Him. As a daddy, I love it when I come home and hear the glee in my children's voices; nothing compares to the rapid footsteps coming near to me. This day, Adam and Eve don't run to meet their Father. He knows something is terribly wrong. He knows Adam and Eve will never be the same again and neither will their relationship with Him.

Adam and Eve were hiding, and they weren't playing a game. Fear and shame took control. These two powerful emotions overwhelmed them to the point where they hid from the one who had fearfully and wonderfully made them. For the first time ever, they were afraid to be with God. Dreadfully, Satan robbed humanity of their very purpose—to be with God.

Fear overtakes us with irrational thoughts, haunting us and keeping us away from the people we should be with and the places we should be. How has fear impacted you? What dreams have you surrendered? What opportunities have you bypassed? What relationships have you wrecked all because of fear? This powerful force is at work in us and keeps us from becoming who God wants us to be.

I remember once, at the end of my college career, I was presented with the opportunity to attend a prestigious university in order to pursue my master's degree. I was offered a 75% scholarship. As the puppet of fear, I shamefully rejected this honor. Fear stole it from me. I gave up a wonderful opportunity due to my allegiance to fear. My fear, however, was not a fear that you might expect. It was a fear of success. Wait. Let me explain. I feared becoming a success because if I failed as a success, it would be worse than if I failed as an average guy. Fear makes no sense. Fear just steals, kills, and destroys. It is the brainchild of your enemy.

Excuses Justified Their Actions

The next evil that surfaced was humanity's unwillingness to take responsibility for their actions. A victim mindset seemed so reasonable. After the Fall, the man answered first. Adam's response to God is revealing to say the least. He said, "The woman YOU gave me gave me the fruit to eat." He immediately made excuses and cast the blame on someone else. In this case, he blamed Eve *and* God. Excuses grant us no power to move forward. Instead, we are to be responsible, or as my professor would say, we need to be "response-able." We were created to be able to respond correctly. Excuses and blaming others forfeits our place of responsibility. We recognize this as a poison that entered humanity at the Fall because Eve responded the same way—except her blame was toward the serpent. She said, "The serpent deceived me and I ate." The problem with casting blame is that it doesn't fix or solve your condition.

Blame is the root of a victim mentality. We become content with brokenness and entrapped in a life of mediocrity. Rather than searching for a solution and finding a way of escape, we simply hunker down in our shame, hide in our fear, and then blame others for our condition. The way of escape from our past is never found through "passing the buck." Your divine DNA must be unlocked.

Judgments Turned Their Blessings into Curses

Lastly, judgments were distributed as a result of the Fall. This was the fall from glory. God had to relate differently to His creation, His children, for the first time. This was not His original intention, but due to sin, it was the new reality. God judged humanity and the serpent. Dreadfully, this one act of man impacted all of life, all of future humanity, and even non-human things. Judgment resulted in specific consequences to each created being connected to the Fall. Trying to control the impact of sin is like trying to catch water in a fishing net. It cannot be contained.

In the next chapter, we are going to review the Fallout—what has happened TO YOU. Recognizing the impact of the Fall in your daily journey will help you escape the past as you move forward in your life. The power of lies resides in their hiddenness. Prepare for lies to be exposed that will give you the keys to unlock your divine DNA and enter your future today!

CHAPTER 4
THE FALLOUT
WHAT HAPPENED TO YOU

The Fall, which stained humanity on the inside, has also impacted the way humanity fleshes life out. As a result of fear, shame, and a victim mentality, we find ourselves expressing behaviors, experiencing hardships, and failing in life. The loss of glory due to sin left humanity without the divine DNA in full operation. The loss of blessing, lack of increase, loss of position, broken relationships, and a forfeited purpose leads to a grossly distorted reflection of God. This loss cultivates a life of defeat. This is not what God intended. Sin touches all of life. Everything about humanity was impacted by this poison.

We can embrace our true identity if we understand the attributes that make us a person. Our personhood is expressed in many different ways. Dr. Wes Pinkham identifies seven elements in particular that are intimately connected to our existence as humans[5]. A person is a created, spiritual, physical, historical, rational, valuing, and social being[6]. These seven areas affirm that you are a person, a human. These seven aspects blend together to create your personhood. It is these seven things, masterfully combined together, that form and shape that unique person called *you*. Accordingly, our personal identity is how we interpret these aspects in our lives.

Our enemy takes and perverts our perception of these aspects and takes advantage of the brokenness within our being. **We are born broken.** Every single person is born with a damaged nature. This brokenness leads us to misinterpreting our true selves and misusing our humanity—just like trying to use a hair dryer for something other than drying hair. It might blow hot air, but when used wrongly, what it touches might be damaged. Next, this brokenness spills over into the lives of those around us. You have heard the saying "hurt people hurt people." This is the problem with life in a shattered world. It is being ordered and lived out by people who have been broken by the Fall. These aspects of your being have been distorted through sin. Let's talk about each one and how these components are meant to be expressed.

A Created Being

Isn't this thought a little unnecessary? Of course we are created beings. But think about it. Your value, the validity of your being, is directly related to the fact that God created you. God wanted you here, now. You are not an accident. You are a masterpiece conceived in the heart of Almighty God. You are special because God created you. You are supposed to be here—right now. You are here because God decreed for you to be here. You are a person because God decreed you to be a person. Let that sink in just for a moment.

Sadly, sin locked up an incredible divine DNA within you. When our understanding of who we are is distorted, all kinds of nasty things can happen. Government can say you are insignificant and therefore do not deserve to exist because your mother doesn't want you—a.k.a. abortion. You and your family can say that you are too much of a hardship in your failing days and determine it is better to end your life early with medicine—a.k.a. euthanasia. When we don't understand this reality, we are reduced wrongfully to an "accident" or a nuisance of our mother and father. We perhaps see ourselves as the mere result of a chance collision in the universe that somehow caused what we are now.

A Spiritual Being

Understanding that you are a spiritual being is important to truly understand potential and capacity in life. You are created with the capacity to connect with a reality beyond what we can see. This is the part that died instantly in the Garden. Sin killed this part of humanity. You were created as a body, soul, and spirit. Sin so fractured your being that you are only born with two-thirds of your function. Sadly, this two-thirds is dysfunctional without Christ. The spirit is what connects you to God. When we are "dead in sin," our lives are reduced to our earthly experience—how and what we feel, think, or desire. Our decisions and determinations are made through our relationship with our bodies and our souls. This is our reality. Unfortunately, this is inadequate. The problem is that our bodies and our souls have no ability to become what we were created by God to be. Until we unlock our divine DNA, our true identities are trapped inside a world of disorder. You are, in essence, the expression of only two parts of a tripartite being. How does this impact you? You learn to do what "feels good." You interpret who you are by your "feelings," emotions that are diseased by brokenness and deception. The sin within you creates desires for things that ultimately are meant to destroy. It is the "fruit failure" all over again. You crave what will kill you.

A Physical Being

I touched on this above. You have a physical body. This is important in order for you to be you. Your body houses the true you, but it is only a part of who you are. Sin causes us to disrespect this aspect of our being. We fail to exercise. We eat poorly. We consume substances that alter the present moment in hopes to change or, at least, numb reality. We join our bodies in sexual encounters that are outside the parameters God established for human experience. All of these misuses impact us. Your body is intimately connected to your soul and your soul to your spirit. You cannot separate them. In Western culture, we objectify everything. We believe that somehow we can divide our private life from our public life. We think it is possible to disregard our physical needs and that it will not impact the rest of our being. We know this is impossible, but we try it. We don't get rest, we don't take care of ourselves, and then we wonder why we make bad decisions and have no energy to pursue our dreams. Our bodies are one of the vital parts of who we are, and they must be honored.

The physical being is important. Notice how God feels about our bodies. Paul, relating the mind of God, says, "If anyone destroys God's temple, God will destroy him. For God's temple is holy, and you are that temple" (1 Corinthians 3:16). In the Old Testament, God illustrates how significant our bodies are by comparing them to Him. "Whoever sheds the blood of man, by man shall his blood be shed, for God made man in his own image" (Genesis 9:6). Your body, in some mysterious way, is a literal reflection of God's image.

A Historical Being

You have a place in history, but the Fallout of sin robs you of your significance. Missed opportunities, failures, and errors in judgment come as a thief and cause you to shipwreck your purpose. You were created for this time. Unfortunately, the fallout of sin leaves you in a place where you feel disqualified. You give up and settle for a life of mediocrity, and tragically, some have lost (or even ended) their lives far earlier than their "appointed time to die" (See Hebrews 9:27). God determined for you to be born, and He has appointed a day for your death. You have a history. The Fallout threatens to erase the pages of His story for you. The great psalmist David penned these words in Psalm 139:16: "Your eyes saw my unformed substance; in your book were written, every one of them, the days that were formed for me, when as yet there was none of them." There is a book written, and its title is (write your name here: _____). The book has your name on it. There is only one copy in existence. When you discover your divine DNA, you discover your potential. Your destiny is already established in the heavenly places, but the Fallout threatens your ability to discover how to transfer what God has said about you into the present realm.

A Rational Being

God created us to reason. This is part of being created in His likeness. He didn't intend for us to exist like robots without the ability to make choices and to establish structures and systems that help order life. You are created to be "response-able."[7] Remember, God placed man here to steward the earth. His intention was for us to be able to think like Him and to make decisions like He would. The Fallout perverted our reason as well. Since our spirits were dead, reason was reduced to merely physical and soulish aspects of our being. Reason became driven by the here and now and the feeling of the moment. Perverted reason creates all kinds of chaos and environment for destruction. Brokenness, hatred, and fear establish a world full of war, violence, and misplaced dominion. Governments rationalize injustice. The judicial branch reasons away divine truth. "Fallen" reason is a runaway train on a track to hell. We reason our way into addictions, divorces, failures, and shameful regrets. They each had a reason. The serpent gave a reason to eat the fruit. The problem is that the reason was distorted with a half-truth. A half-truth is the first step to becoming enslaved to a lie. Half-truths lock up your divine DNA. Each time you fail or find yourself defeated and feel that struggle within, it is your divine DNA crying out to be released!

A Valuing Being

Recognizing that we are created, spiritual, physical, historical, and rational beings, it is not difficult to see that we have value. To value something means to establish the importance, worth, or usefulness of something. The Fallout creates confusion on this concept of value. Why is value important? You invest in what you value. You give your time, energy, and money to things—and parts of life—that you value. The problem with value gone awry is that your life is given to things that are not worth your destiny. The Fallout leads you to a place of giving your life to activities that are less than your worth.

Value is driven by our understanding. The serpent convinced Eve there was something of value to her in the fruit. His persuasion caused her to think that she was missing something and that this fruit (more than all the others) could satisfy her.

I remember when I was kid and didn't understand value. I had a beautiful baseball, and I decided to take it to school with me one day. On the bus ride home, one of the older kids unintentionally taught me a lesson on value. He convinced me to trade my "smaller, less significant" baseball for his "bigger, better" softball. He persuaded me that size was the determiner of value. I didn't realize my baseball was better than the softball. I believed a lie about value, and it caused me to trade something more for something less.

You will protect and fight for what you value. Value, when driven by lies and perversion, creates the opportunity for treasures to be lost and valuables to be pilfered. How have distorted values impacted you? Did you get involved in a relationship you shouldn't have been in? Have you been enslaved by debt that haunts you? Perhaps you lost your virginity, or found yourself with a criminal record, or were estranged from someone significant in your life. The Fallout causes us to invest our lives into "stocks" of death.

A Social Being

You were created for relationships. A human's wholeness is established and dependent on healthy, life-giving connections with others, but the Fallout assaulted this aspect of our existence. Adam and Eve, intended by God to dwell together in perfect unity, were reduced, at best, to merely existing together. The social reality bruised by sin became a danger zone. In its worst form, fathers abandon their children. Mothers lose their minds and kill their babies. Husbands and wives go from best friends to violent enemies. The sin within us takes what God meant to complete us and instead causes our relationships to deplete us. **Sin always reverses the blessing and invokes a curse.**

Not only does the Fallout cause our connections to harm us but the enemy has initiated a plan to disconnect us completely so that healing isn't available. Even our virtual world threatens to disconnect us by creating a place of "no touch." Our relationships and, not insignificantly, our ability to touch and be touched in a healthy way must not be neglected. As Maria Konnikova notes, "Touch is the first of the senses to develop in the human infant."[8] As far back as the 1940s, an observation by R.A. Spitz noted the power of touch. He reported that German homes experienced high mortality rates even when all the basic needs were provided. The cause was given as a lack of touch for the babies.[9] We are created to be touched. We are created to be connected to others.

Children are said to even need four hugs a day just to survive![10] We are created for interdependence and not independence.

Each of these realities of personhood have in some way been touched by the Fall. The Fallout in your life means that you express the aspects of personhood in ways that are perverted, confused, and dysfunctional. Broken marriages, perverted sexuality, homosexuality, murder, depression…the list goes on and on. You would quit reading if I named every dysfunction of humankind. But then again, this seems to be what sells on the nightly news. This evil part of the fallen human condition plagues all of us.

If I had the privilege to sit down with you and listen to your struggles and setbacks in life, and we were able to talk about the areas of your own identity where you are confused or struggling, I could answer and say, "This is the Fallout caused by that first bad day for humanity."

Is it hopeless?

Are you destined to always live below your intended purpose?

Is this the plight humanity is condemned to?

Will you ever escape the past and unlock your divine DNA?

I have good news! There is a way—a road God has paved to lead you to where you are supposed to be. There is a journey of transformation that creates the opportunity for you to escape yesterday and fully embrace your true identity. Let me introduce you to the Fall Guy.

CHAPTER 5
THE FALL GUY
WHAT HAPPENED FOR YOU

We looked at the Fall and saw how sin afflicted humanity like a poison deep within. We discussed the Fallout and how this sinful nature has impacted everything around us. If this was the end of the story, we would be a hopeless people with nothing to look forward to in the future. I would have to look you in the eye and say, "Give up—there's no use to even try!" But thankfully this is not the end! I have an answer to whatever you are dealing with. Gratefully, there is hope because of the Fall Guy! God, who is never too far from us, saw the human condition and felt compassion. Listen to His response as He reviewed our predicament:

> *For God so loved the world, that he gave his only Son, that whoever believes in him should not perish but have eternal life.* (John 3:16)

God didn't give up on us. If you have ever had anything that you invested a lot of money and time into, then you know how hard it is to let it go. You will fight for it. You will expend every cost in order to save it if it is in danger. If it is a child, you will search out every doctor and explore every medical solution. God looked at us and said, "I have to do something about this!"

This is only fitting considering how much He loves you. There is no limit to His love, and as a result, there is no limit to His effort to save us.

You are that important to Him. To save us from sin, from ourselves, and from the schemes of our enemy, He held back nothing. He sent Jesus, His only Son, to be the Fall Guy. A fall guy is simply a "scapegoat." In our understanding, we know the fall guy as the one who takes the fall for everyone else. The implication is that someone, or many others, may be to blame but only one receives the punishment. Did you know that this concept is a biblical concept? Jesus was the first Fall Guy.

In Leviticus 16, we learn where this idea of a scapegoat, a fall guy, originated. It's important to remember when we look at the Old Testament, which can seem dated and irrelevant to our modern culture, that we must look for the principle behind the story. In this case, we see that God established the Law to govern the behaviors and interactions between people. Prior to the day Adam and Eve sinned, God instituted a plan to bring about a story of redemption.

God implemented an entire system (i.e., the Law), which would reveal two things. First, humans were incapable of living as He intended. Sin had rendered us powerless. The Fall and the Fallout were too great for us to overcome on our own, and the Law taught humanity that they needed help. Secondly, the Law would teach us how our redemption would come. Sin has to be dealt with. Sin cannot be overlooked or dismissed. It will not go away on its own.

Thus, our story in Leviticus reveals that God had a plan. The priest provided two goats to address the sin problem. One would be killed. The other would have all the sins of the people pronounced on it, and then it would be sent into the wilderness alive. It represented the goat taking the sins of the people upon itself, and then it would be sent away. This is a powerful message because the people deserved to be punished for their sin, but the goat was a substitute for them. Accordingly, humans could go on living as if they had not committed those sins. They could live without the punishment for their sins.

The Fall Guy, Jesus, is your scapegoat. He is your substitute. In the Old Testament, it took two goats to represent man's sin. One was killed, and the other illustrated the sin being taken away. In Jesus, there was no need for two actions. In Him, both works of redemption were employed. Read these scriptures as you escape your past by accepting what Jesus did for you!

> *For our sake he made him to be sin who knew no sin, so that in him we might become the righteousness of God.* (2 Corinthians 5:21)

> *He himself bore our sins in his body on the tree, that we might die to sin and live to righteousness. By his wounds you have been healed.* (1 Peter 2:24)

Pastor John Gray said it like this: "Jesus didn't die for you; He died AS you!"[35]

Just as the Fallout touches all of humanity, the Fall Guy is available to all of humanity. No one is beyond His reach.

I invite you to accept this personally. Whatever has held you back and whatever has disqualified you, Jesus has paid the price. He became YOUR Fall Guy. He has made it possible to truly unlock your divine DNA. You are free to live as God intended! Let's go get it!

If you have never accepted Jesus as your Lord and Savior or perhaps you have fallen away from a relationship with Him it is time to use your first key. The first key is putting your trust in God. It is isn't hard. It isn't complicated. You don't have to do anything except believe in your Fall Guy. Here is a simple prayer that will help you take the first step in unlocking your divine DNA. Pray this and believe it in your heart and you will be set free:

"Father God, I acknowledge that you sent Jesus as my Fall Guy. I trust that He has done everything for me. He has forgiven my sins. He has paid the price for my mistakes. Jesus, I confess that you are Lord of my life. I confess that you died on a cross and rose from the dead and now you have the keys that will set me free from my past. Today, I commit to unlocking my divine DNA with the keys of your kingdom! Thank you for making everything new!

If you prayed that prayer I want to get you the tools necessary to support your relationship with Jesus Christ. Go to our website, www.tonycolson.com, and click on the link, "Ready for the First Key" and then complete the online form. We will get you started on the right track. Congratulations on taking the first step in unlocking your divine DNA!

PART TWO

EMBRACING YOUR IDENTITY

CHAPTER 6
YOUR DIVINE DNA: BLESSING
THE SOURCE OF GLORY

"They've got what it takes!" This statement is made about people that seem to rise above difficulties, those that achieve greatness when others are at best mediocre, and those that tend to always come out with the victory. It is as if they have some kind of advantage, some kind of superpower that leaves everyone else lacking. Something tells me that since you are reading this book, you believe there is more in you as well. You want to be one of those individuals that excel in life. You believe you are meant to thrive and not barely survive. I am here to confirm that <u>YOU</u> have what it takes. The divine DNA within you has the potential to achieve greatness and to fulfill your destiny. I want you to discover it today. I want you to see what is already there. Your divine DNA is waiting to be released; waiting to be revealed to this world. Too often we live from our past rather than the future God has planned for us. In order to enter your future, you must embrace your true identity. It is time for you to take the keys and unlock your divine DNA! Put your trust in the Fall Guy, Jesus, so you can be everything you were created to be.

The very first lesson that you need to adopt in order to embrace your true identity is to realize that you have what it takes *right now*. Fulfilling potential is not something that becomes possible after a person finds all the right resources and gains each piece of the missing information. Potential is first activated when one accepts the fact that what they need is already within them.

The Apostle Paul made a statement that reveals a key to living life to the full. He says that God has blessed us with every spiritual blessing in the heavenly places (See Ephesians 1:3). This declaration is in the past tense. It is an action that has already occurred. Add this thought to the words of the great founding father of the Church, Peter, who said that we have everything we need for life and godliness, and you have a revelation that is fueled with potential (See 2 Peter 1:3). Both of these statements are past tense realities. Right now, you have every key you need to unlock your divine DNA. I want you to go look at yourself in the mirror and declare, "I have what it takes right now!" Go do it…I will wait for you! Declare to yourself, "I have what it takes right now!"

Paul uncovered this ancient mystery when He declared, "Christ in you, the hope of glory" (Colossians 1:27). When you accepted Christ, He initiated the unlock feature for your divine DNA. Jesus is the unlock code that gives access to your full potential. He comes and awakens your spirit, and your spirit is then freed to become everything that

God intended for you to be—His original you! Jesus, the express image of God, began the process of repairing your ability to reflect His glory in the earth. The key to living life to the full, then, is to connect your spirit to the heavenly resources already available.

You have what it takes. You have what it takes because God Himself has—past tense—already blessed you with everything you need to unlock the divine DNA. In order to tap into your blessings, let's look at the nature of blessing so that you can best embrace its work in your life. Remember, the goal of this book is to help you see that God's original intention for humanity is the same intention He has for you. In Genesis 1:28, the scripture declares that God blessed the first man and woman. This is the difference maker! This is what empowers you to walk in the other four components of the divine DNA. The blessing of God enables you to step into what otherwise is impossible. When you understand that God Himself has declared a blessing over your life, then you can escape your past, embrace your true identity, and enter your future.

There are two significant words in the Bible that express "blessing." One word is found in the Old Testament and the other in the New Testament. The Old Testament word for blessing is "barak." This word simply means to kneel or to bless. The imagery is that the one being blessed is kneeling down before the one doing the blessing. This shows the dependence that the one being blessed has on the one doing the blessing. It can also illustrate that the one who is doing the blessing is greater than the one being blessed.

In the New Testament, the Greek word "eulogeo" is used. It is the combination of two words: "eu" and "logos." *Eu* means well or good, while *logos* means word or reason. When joining these two words together to find our meaning, we see that when God blesses us, He is declaring over our lives a good word. Why is this so significant? Remember, this is the same way that God spoke creation into existence. God called light out of darkness. He called order out of chaos. He made something out of nothing. This same God looks at your life, no matter how He found you, and blesses you with a declaration. He speaks a good word over you that has the power to recreate your reality. His Word never returns void (See Isaiah 55:11). His Word has authority over everything. His Word is the difference maker and has already been decreed in the heavenly places on your behalf. There is power in His Word!

As we discovered in the Fall, the blessing was replaced with a curse when the first man chose to disobey. It so impacted our nature that God's intention for humanity was severely affected. It left humanity with no power to regain its place. Death entered our lives. Thankfully, we learned that Jesus came as the Fall Guy and implemented the opportunity for us to recover our lost capacity. This "good news" is what we call the Gospel. It is the story of Christ. When you accept Jesus into your life, you accept the power of blessing into your life. Jesus is the Word that rewrites your story. His act of obedience on the cross creates the opportunity for your curse to be changed to blessing.

In the book of John, we learn that the same Word that was present at creation is the same Word that came and lived on the earth in human form. Jesus is the *logos*. This Word from God came to set in motion the power of blessing in our lives. In John 1:14, the scripture says, "The Word became flesh and dwelt among us, and we have beheld his glory, glory as of the only Son from the

Father, full of grace and truth." The blessing came from heaven and has made a way for you and me to embrace our true identity. This Word has two components: grace and truth.

Perhaps you have heard grace defined as unmerited favor. It simply means that there is nothing that you have done, or could do, that could earn salvation. Grace is something that you don't deserve. But there is something more to grace that you need to understand. Your need for grace doesn't end when you accept Christ. Being born-again actually opens the door of grace to function as it should. I want you to see grace in the following way; Grace is "a heavenly resource to meet an earthly need." Jesus had access to all of heaven's resources. Grace satisfied everything that He needed in order to fulfill His purpose. Jesus went to the cross and made a way for you and me to step into our full purpose. There is nothing else that needs to be done by God in order for you to become the you He intended. The essential step that remains for grace to be transferred into your life is for you to embrace your blessings.

Truth is the second aspect of what Christ revealed in His coming. He brought truth and when you know the truth, the truth will make you free (See John 8:32). Truth is not something that has to be created. Truth is what already is. It is a past tense reality that continues to exist in the present. You are already blessed. You are already qualified. You are already capable of rising to your potential. Christ said, "It is finished." It accomplished the work that needed to be done for you. Your divine DNA is already in you; it is merely waiting to be revealed to the world. You have what it takes. You have the difference maker dwelling inside of you. Jesus is the "eu"-"logos," the good word, and He dwells inside of you! Grace and truth are working together in order to transfer heaven's reality into your existence.

If this good word has already been spoken about us, why do so many of us continue to live in bondage, in brokenness, and in less than our intended glory? Most of us have not learned how to activate blessing in our lives. We don't understand that it does require something from us in order to release grace into the earth. Jesus taught His disciples to pray like this: "Your kingdom come, Your will be done on earth as it is in heaven." (Matthew 6: 10) Did you catch it? Jesus taught us to declare heaven's reality to come into the earth. You have to agree with what God has already spoken. Jesus has made it possible, but you have to seize it. The Apostle Paul appeals to us not to receive the grace of God in vain (See 2 Corinthians 6:1). This implies that some of us can miss what God has prepared for us. Remember, grace is a heavenly resource to meet an earthly need, yet there are some of us that will never seize it. We miss it. We live life saved but not full. We will be survivors but not thrivers. We will be victims and not victors. We will barely make it rather than bravely take it.

God has made available every resource and has made possible everything necessary for you to unlock your divine DNA. God's blessing is the difference maker. The key, then, is to learn how to seize the blessing. The blessing is the "good word" that includes both grace and truth, and it has the power to transfer heaven's reality into the earth. We are going to talk more about this divine transfer later, but for now, realize that in order to seize your blessing, you have to seed your blessing.

In Luke 8, we learn that God's Word is a seed (See Luke 8:4–15). This means that the Word in and of itself is not your harvest. It is the potential of your harvest.

Your enemy understands the threat that God's Word has on his plans, and he doesn't want you to embrace the seed into your life. In Luke's account, we see that there are many enemies of the seed. Seeds do not produce a harvest unless they are given the opportunity to grow. Your divine DNA will never arrive unless you give the seed, the Word of God, the proper opportunity to produce its harvest of blessing into your life. The blessing has already been decreed, but it has to be seized. The seed has to be planted, protected, and patiently waited on.

During this time of transfer from heaven to the earth, the seed faces the following challenges. First, the enemy himself will come and rob the seed from your life. He does this by "trampling" the seed with accusations, arguments, and imaginations that cause you to abandon the Word of God from your life. This is the same strategy that we recognized from the serpent when he schemed against Eve. The enemy will send people into your life that stomp on your revelation of God's Word. God will speak to you about a change you need to make, a habit you need to break, a pattern you need to embrace, or a process that you need to employ. Then the enemy will send that "friend" or foe that reasons with you on why you should do the opposite. He will bring a person that you really trust or greatly admire into your life, and they will propose an idea that is contrary to the seed. Sometimes that enemy is yourself. This is your enemy's way of walking on your destiny. He steals the Word so he can prevent your divine DNA from showing up.

Other things threaten the seed as well. According to our parable, some seeds are destroyed during times of testing. When life gets difficult, we abandon the truth of God's Word in order to find a place of comfort. We desert our commitment to protect the seed until harvest time because we see an easier way. This forfeits our destiny without us ever realizing it. As Craig Groeschel says, "Sometimes the difference between where you are and where God wants you to be is the pain that you are unwilling to endure."[11]

How about you? In what ways have you forfeited your divine DNA in the tests of life? Perhaps it was a job opportunity that God was wanting to give you, but you chose to go a dishonest route. Perhaps there is a blessing of healing waiting to be released into your life, but you have been unwilling to exercise or eat properly in order to activate that miracle. You have to seed it. You have to seize it. It is time to receive God's grace in full. It is time for you to operate with all of your divine DNA.

Lastly, God gives you His DNA not simply to make your life better or greater or easier. The divine DNA of blessing is meant to empower you to become a blessing. As Robert Sheppard said, "You are blessed to be a blessing."[36] The father of faith, Abraham, who was given the great covenant of blessing, was told in Genesis 12 that God would bless him and make him great in order that he might be a blessing. It is the same principle that we are to be a reflection of God in the earth. We are not to just be consumers but givers. We are not to walk with a "just enough" mindset but with a "more than enough" mentality. When you are blessed, you can bless others. God has declared for you to be the head and not the tail (See Deuteronomy 28:13). When you live life from a perspective of prosperity, it is a normal thing to add value to the people around you. As a Christian, you should be a person of resources, creativity, and blessing! The divine DNA of blessing enables you to become the image of God in the earth. His blessing empowers you to be like Him in the earth. The blessing of the Lord brings permission, potential, and position.

> Permission – Access
> Potential – Ability
> Position – Authority

Permission is granted to people who have the right to gain access. When I go to my office, I have been given a key to gain access. The key is my permission to enter. You have been given permission to access God's presence. Hebrews 4:16 says, "Let us then with confidence draw near to the throne of grace, that we may receive mercy and find grace to help in time of need." Notice the phrase "throne of grace"—isn't that powerful? Because of your relationship with God, you have access to approach His throne of grace.

First of all, a throne is the place where a ruler of a kingdom sits. God has granted you access into the place where He makes decisions, and you can enter that place where He rules over all things. Don't miss it. I am talking about you. Yes, YOU! You have permission to approach God's place of authority so that His Kingdom can be released into your life. He has called you to rule a domain here in the same way He rules there. How? Through grace. It is a throne of grace. Grace is a heavenly resource to meet an earthly need, and you have access to everything you need to succeed in life.

This access to grace then empowers you to fulfill your potential in life. Potential to succeed and not to fail. Potential to rule and not be enslaved. Potential to increase and not decrease. You have heavenly potential in this earthly realm. I am going to keep saying it over and over until you get it. "As a man thinks, so he is."

You are empowered through grace to fulfill your divine destiny. In other words, the power for you to be like God is inside you right now. There is nothing impossible for those who are in Christ.

The third blessing is a position of authority. When you accepted Christ, He gave you the "right" to become a son or daughter of God (John 1:12). Secondly, the Apostle Paul says you have been "seated" with Him (See Ephesians 2:6). God welcomes you to sit down in that position of grace. It is not something that you walk in and out of. The grace is always available for any need. Grace is not something that you have to beg for. You have been given a position of grace, and this mindset will change the way you approach everything. Your expectations will begin to conform to God's expectations. As you grow in your relationship with God, you begin to think like Him, feel like Him, and desire like Him. It is an awesome transformation from glory to glory.

You are blessed with every spiritual blessing in the heavenly places and, as a result, have permission to embrace your true identity. You have permission to escape the past. You have permission to move forward and let go of the shame. The blessing also grants potential, however, and you have the power to conquer that bad habit. You have the power to let go of that relationship. You have the power to walk in victory in every area of your life. You have what it takes in all areas of your life and godliness.

Lastly, the blessing of the Lord positions you to be the reflection of God in the earth. You are "seated" with Christ in heavenly places (See Ephesians 2:6). You have permission, you have power, and you have position to unlock your divine DNA. This blessing on your life transforms you into more than a conqueror (See Romans 8:37). I love this phrase. The Apostle Paul could have just said, "You are a conqueror," and we would have gotten excited. But he says, "You are more than a conqueror." This indicates that the enemies that you defeat are not going to have the opportunity to resurface. You are going to rule over your enemies, and you are going to take back the land the enemy stole from you. You are more than a conqueror. The blessing of God creates the opportunity for you to be fruitful, to have dominion, to enjoy healthy relationships, and to fulfill your purpose. As you seize your blessing, you can embrace the next component of your divine DNA: fruitfulness.

CHAPTER 7
YOUR DIVINE DNA: INCREASE
THE EXPECTATION OF GLORY

Do you like to go shopping? Let me say it a little differently. What if I said to you that I was going to give you a blank check and you could go to any store you would like and buy anything you wanted—would you get excited about that? Now what if I invited you on a window shopping trip. You have no money. You can only go look at items through a wall of glass. Window shopping just doesn't sound as appealing, does it?

Does anyone ever really like window shopping over an actual shopping spree? You know the drill. You go to a store that you really like, and you longingly gaze in from the outside—through a window—and wish that you could afford the item on the other side. You are within feet, and sometimes inches, of that item that you really want. And yet you walk away hoping your situation changes in the future.

Unfortunately, many of us "window shop" through life. We are plagued by this "not enough" mentality. It impacts so many of us. How about you? Have you been peering through the window of life wishing you had what was on the other side? Perhaps you have checked your resources and think you don't have what it takes to thrive. You see all those people on the "other side" with the right stuff. You dream of a different life, but you never seem to be able to obtain it. You hope for a different place in life but never seem to arrive. I am here to challenge you to do a faith check. What would it take for you to acquire the goal? "What it takes" may be more money, different friends, additional resources, increased _____. You fill in the blank. What is your reason? What keeps you stuck on the outside looking in?

I want to introduce you to a new approach to life. I am here to declare to you that you already have what it takes. I am here to cheer you on and say, "You can do better than that," because there is more in you. When you accepted Jesus Christ, your capacity changed. You are no longer condemned by the same decrees we learned about through the Fall. The Fallout should no longer be your destiny. Your divine DNA gives you the capacity to move out of the place where you are, to rise above your current circumstances, and to overcome that intimidating mountain in your way. You can do better because you were created with a divine component called increase.

You have permission.
You have potential.
You have position.

Once activated, mediocrity and lack have to submit to these driving forces. God's original intention for mankind was for you to multiply and to be fruitful. The very cells in our body affirm this divinely influenced reality.

Kirstie Saltsman says it like this: "Each of us began as a single cell. This cell couldn't move, think, see, or do things like laugh and talk. But the one thing it could do, and do very well, was divide—and divide it did. The lone cell became two, and then four, then eight and so on, in time becoming the amazing person that is you. Think of how far you've come. You can laugh at a joke, stand on your head, read a book, eat an ice cream cone, hear a symphony, and do countless other things."[34]

Even though you began as one cell, you were created with an innate capacity to increase. The spirit of multiplication transformed the singleness of one cell into a masterpiece of cell composition. This is what we now call "you." You are a fearfully and wonderfully made work of genius, crafted by the very hand of God. The same God who looked into chaos and demanded order…the same God who spoke into darkness and called out light…this same God formed you from a single thought. That one thought became a word, which was birthed into the earthly realm. That one thought became a divinely inspired story written by the hand of God. You are created to increase.

But although we were created to increase, we also struggle with failure at times. The Apostle Peter had insight into failure. He was always sticking his foot in his mouth and finding himself at odds with Jesus. His passion and good intentions were haunted by a fallen human nature. Jesus, on multiple occasions, had to correct this fisherman with an overarching boldness. On one occurrence, Jesus rebuked Peter literally by saying, "Get behind me, Satan!" (Matthew 16:23). It was also

Peter who vehemently denied Jesus by using profanity in order to make his lie more believable. And yet, one day, Peter understood that through Christ even terrible sinners and people prone to failure can change.

Jesus changed this broken, messed up Peter into a man of God who became a powerful preacher. He blossomed into the first leader of the Church. Think about that. This man, whom Jesus had to continually clean up messes after, was chosen to be the founding father of the Church! Peter had learned to quit window shopping. He gave up living with a poverty mindset. He learned that when Jesus comes into your life, everything changes. What was once impossible because of the Fall is now possible because of the Fall Guy! Peter came to realize his potential in life was not dependent upon his own strength; his divine DNA contained increase. Increase should be natural to the believer. It was in Peter's nature. It is in YOUR nature. "His divine power has granted to us all things that pertain to life and godliness, through the knowledge of Him who called us to his own glory and excellence" (2 Peter 1:3). You have everything you need right now! The resources, the gifting, the capacity, and the power to change your life are available right now! You were created to increase. You were created to express glory and excellence.

An important thing for you to understand is that this capacity and potential do not just refer to your spirituality or godliness. Oftentimes we reduce our relationship with God to a church service or just spiritual moments. According to Peter, this power was given—past tense—for EVERYTHING that pertains to life and godliness. This means that God is at work for you in every aspect of your life. Jesus didn't come to just make you "godly" so you could get into heaven. He came to give you life and life to the full. He came to restore your capacity to be His image in the earth in every area of life. You have the divine DNA to be a better spouse, a better parent, a better employee, or a better boss.

The Model of Increase

Too often we distance ourselves from the life that Jesus lived on the earth. It is a fact that Jesus is 100% God. Nevertheless, we need to understand that Jesus was not expressing life on earth as God but rather living out life as a human. He became a human like you and I. As we learned earlier, He was the Fall Guy for us. But there was more at work than accomplishing the work of salvation for us. He was also modeling life as God intends humanity to live—ON THE EARTH.

You might say that is ridiculous. There is no way that God wants humans to be like God. Yet this is exactly what He created humans to be (See Leviticus 11:44). We were created in His image, and we were created according to His likeness. Jesus, in order to demonstrate for us this original intention for man, did something unbelievable. He came to this earth and lived as a man. The Apostle Paul explains this reality in the second chapter of Philippians, verses 5–7:

> *Make your own attitude that of Christ Jesus, who, existing in the form of God, did not consider equality with God as something to be used for His own advantage. Instead He emptied Himself by assuming the form of a slave, taking on the likeness of men.* (Philippians 2:5-7 HCSB)

Isn't that incredible? Jesus emptied Himself of divine privilege in order to walk on earth like you and I. He did this to take our place—as the Fall Guy—but also to restore our place. He was defeated so we could win. He gave up His rights so we could get our rights back.

Jesus was not acting like God. He was acting like a man reflecting God. He came to show us how to live. I want to show you something incredible in the Scriptures. Perhaps this will help you see that He came and lived like we are supposed to live. Read this verse slowly: "And Jesus increased in wisdom and in stature and in favor with God and man" (Luke 2:52). Did you catch it? Jesus increased! Yes, the Son of God increased.

There are three areas in which Jesus increased. We understand that He was born and therefore entered this world as a baby through the natural process of childbirth. It is understandable, then, to recognize that Jesus grew physically—in stature.

Secondly, we see that Jesus increased in wisdom. Wisdom can be defined as the ability to use knowledge effectively. Jesus found himself in the temple at age 12 confounding the scholars and the teachers of the Law. He had wisdom that granted Him the ability to use the knowledge that He had. Amazingly, Jesus didn't come into the world with wisdom pre-packaged. He grew in wisdom. Day by day, year by year, He become wiser and wiser.

The third aspect of increase in Jesus' life is possibly the most profound. He increased in favor. And yet not just favor with man. He increased in favor with God. Jesus—the Son of God—increased in favor with God. Wow! Jesus Himself became a human and taught us what to expect in life. This word, favor, is the same word found in Ephesians 2:8 declaring that we are saved by grace. Jesus increased in grace with God. Jesus didn't need to be saved; therefore grace or favor must have an added purpose. Here is my definition. Grace is a heavenly resource to meet an earthly need. Jesus increased in heavenly resources in order to meet His earthly needs and in order to fulfill His divine purpose.

> Grace is a heavenly resource to meet an earthly need.
> Dr. Tony Colson

Through Christ, you are a child of God, and you should expect to increase in wisdom and favor. You should grow in your ability to use knowledge. You should advance in your opportunities with mankind. God should have an increasing disposition toward you. In other words, the way in which God desires to bless you and promote you should increase.

These aspects of increase that we see in the life of Jesus demonstrate that Jesus was our human example of how to live life fully human. Oftentimes we excuse ourselves from the amazing feats and accomplishments of Jesus because, well, he was Jesus. Yet what we must understand is that Jesus came to restore the image of God within us. Increase is part of our created capacity, our divine DNA. The curse has inevitably impacted us physically with the judgment of death that must take place: "And just as it is appointed for a man to die once" (Hebrews 9:27). Each and every one of us will eventually transition into death, but before we bring out the sad music, we can rejoice because this curse of sin was broken completely off our spirits. Our spirits are alive with the opportunity to thrive. When we know the truth, the truth shall make us free. We are free to increase. We are free to multiply.

What does it really matter, you ask? It matters because this spirit of increase should be informing who we are becoming today. The mindset of increase and multiplication should be a part of our thought processes when we are dreaming, planning, and preparing for the next day. This mentality will assault the poverty mindset that enslaves us. The spirit of increase will face our fears of the past and open the doors of our future. Fear says we will fail again like we did last time. Increase says, "This time will be different." It is time to go to the next level.

Remember, Jesus didn't come only to save us from sin. He came to restore the image of God to our lives. He lived His human life as the express image of God. In other words, the way Jesus lived is the expectation God has for your life once you accept Christ. As we step back and observe the life of Christ through this lens, we begin to see something powerful, something that we have never seen before. Yes, we see an awesome Savior. Yes, we see the incredible Son of God. Yes, we see the one who changed everything. But do we see what else is there? Look again. In His life, we should see our potential. In His actions, patterns, and power, we should see our capacity in Him. You can do all things through Christ Jesus (See Philippians 4:13). This is our divine DNA. It is time to unlock it!

You may still be struggling to identify your life with His. Justifiably, you distance yourself from Him. Jesus came to seek and to save those who were lost. This is more than saying, "Jesus came to seek and to save those condemned to hell." Yes, this is part of it. But Jesus came to give direction to those who have lost their way. He is the Way. His example says to you, "You can do better than that," not in a condemning way but in a matter-of-fact way. Jesus understood the capacity of humanity, and He came to demonstrate that capacity.

Jesus knows what is inside you, and He died to pull it out of you!

When His Spirit comes to dwell inside of you, it activates something that was lost—the glorious capacity of increase. Yes, you have it! You *can* do better than that. As a child of God with a new nature, you have a divine capacity to achieve the potential that God originally intended for humanity. You were not born to fall. You were not created to be a victim. There is more in you!

Let's take a journey through the Scriptures in order to solidify this truth in your mind. Most of us are accustomed to a poverty mindset. We are indoctrinated with an understanding that we will never have enough. Our ambitions are faced with what our world has called realities—"That's just the way it is." But I believe you have an advantage. You see, the scorekeeper fixed the game. He created the game. He judges the activities. And He made a way to guarantee your success. This is the power of Jesus Christ. He rewrote the rulebook. The old rulebook said you are broken and will never be enough. The new rulebook says that you have everything that you need for life and godliness. The divine blessing activates the divine increase and creates the opportunity for you to rise to the challenge.

> **The key to increase and capacity is seed.**

First of all, divine increase has to do with one's capacity. It is the ability to adjust to circumstances and respond to difficulties. It is one's ability to meet needs and create change. If you have resources, then you can impact your surroundings. Without resources, dependency is created with debilitating consequences. Divine increase empowers us to be givers and not takers. It positions us as lenders and not borrowers. The key to increase and capacity is seed.

Seed, according to a parable taught by Jesus, was the Word of God (See Matthew 13:1–23). In Genesis 1, when it says that God "blessed" His creation, I believe this was an act of "speaking" into them. This Divine Word was being planted within the creation to activate potential and capacity to fulfill purpose. This Word is a seed that activates increase, dominion, healthy relationships, and purpose. It is vitally important for you to recognize that your DNA has a divine capacity to multiply. You were divinely equip to increase. When we are living as God has intended the natural result should be growth and improvement.

Why is this important? You have to see yourself with a propensity toward wealth and not lack. A poverty mindset will rob you of the expectation that God wants you to operate in.

This Word speaks into your current situation from a posture of "more than enough" rather than lack. Embracing your "identity of increase" will give you the faith to face that mountain, attempt that task you

> "So faith comes from hearing and hearing through the word of Christ." (Romans 10:17)

have been avoiding, go after that career that you thought was unreachable, and so much more! Living from a mindset of multiplication will give you the opportunity to approach that relationship full rather than empty. You relate from a standpoint of contentment and not desperately "needing" that person. We will talk more about relationships but relationships often fail because of false expectations. When you are operating out of a poverty or victim mindset, it is very difficult for you to have healthy relationships. But when you see who you really are in Christ, your approach changes. Actually, everything changes. You have within you the divine DNA of increase.

This increase DNA gives you an advantage. What if you truly expected everything you touched to prosper? What if every project came in on time and under budget and you walked in favor with everyone? Everything that your hands touched you would expect to be successful. You would approach business opportunities with the anticipation that you would be successful. Interviews. Relationships. Doctor's appointments. You name it. This mindset of increase is so important as it determines the way that you approach life. Remember, the way you view yourself determines how you expect life to respond to you.

When we live from a poverty mindset, our posture is to see ourselves dependent upon others to get us where we need to be. When we live from a mindset of increase, we expect life to respond to us. We become sowers rather consumers. We expect life to produce rather than take from us. Kings don't walk through their kingdom dependent upon their people. Good kings are there for their people. We have a domain to steward, and we must see ourselves with the capacity to be successful with it.

The key to this aspect of our journey is to recognize that we have everything we need for life. All of us believe that Jesus was enough for our salvation. We have no trouble believing that what He did on the cross was sufficient to save us from all of our sins.

But I am here to say that the action on the cross by the Fall Guy purchased more than a ticket to heaven. He made possible the opportunity for "increase" to be activated in your life today. Before Jesus, we were dead. You and I had no potential to be who we were created to be. But once you trust the "Fall Guy," everything changes.

You change. You are instantly empowered with the ability to increase and be fruitful. Life is now subject to your purpose. God expects you to increase, and you should expect to increase. You should expect better relationships. You should expect victory over sins. You should expect promotions and favor. You should expect insight and wisdom. God ideas. God opportunities. God stuff. Why? You are His kid! It's in your DNA. You are finally released to function in your created purpose. You were given the right and the power to step into it through Christ. You have permission! You have potential! You have position! You have divine capacity within you to be fruitful and increase so that you are able to fulfill your purpose.

It is time for you to declare the end to your window shopping and get on the other side of the window. Jesus is the door to the other side. He is the way to a better life. Everything you need has already been provided. Use it! Every single resource is waiting for you to employ it. Take it!

Below are five actions that we have to employ in order to release heaven's resources into our earthly experience:

1. Acknowledge God in all your ways.
2. Remain in God all your days.
3. Work hard.
4. Sow seeds.
5. Refuse to give up!

First, you begin by acknowledging your need for God's power and presence in your life. King Solomon taught his readers to acknowledge God in all of their ways so that He would direct their paths (See Proverbs 3:5). The first key to activating the spirit of increase in your life is acknowledging God in all your ways. There is a path to every resource. There is a key to every door. God is the one who grants us access to this path of increase. According to the Apostle Paul, it is God alone who is the provider of increase. You may need to change your view about who supplies all your needs and who your source is. Your employer is NOT your source. You perform acts of labor for them in exchange for a paycheck, but ultimately, you do your work for God, so each day when you wake up, stop and acknowledge Him.

Intentionally and specifically acknowledge that you need God to make the difference in your life. Do you have a job opportunity? Let God know that you need His favor to shine on you in that moment. Do you have a test or an exam? Reach out to God and ask Him for wisdom to be successful. God is the one who grants the increase. Read this powerful truth about God from 1 Chronicles 29:12:

> *Both riches and honor come from you, and you reign over all. In your hand is power and might, and in your hand it is to make great and to give strength to all.* (1 Chronicles 29:12 NKJV)

This is the first step to unlocking the spirit of increase into your life. Your acknowledgement is His welcome into your life. It is as if you open the door into your life so that He can open doors for your life. Personally, each morning when I wake up, I bow on my knees and say this simple prayer: "Father, I acknowledge that I need you to help me be a good son to you, a good husband, a good daddy, and a good pastor, author, and teacher. I invite you to make the difference in these roles that I must fulfill in my life."

Secondly, we must be intentional about remaining in God's Spirit and His Word. This must become a priority in our lives. Jesus Himself offered the guarantee that those who abide in God would be fruitful. You can't acknowledge God and then walk away from Him. You must posture yourself to maintain a right relationship with Him. This involves two things: First, you will need to get His Word in you. His Word is the force that creates, initiates, heals, and produces heavenly intention in the earthly realm. The Word of God is a powerful force in the believer's life. His Word holds everything together.

Secondly, you must also be willing to surrender to His voice and His Word. This keeps you securely in Him. As you are rightfully connected to God and submitted to that Word, it literally causes a divine transfer. In Joshua 1, we learn that the individual that carefully follows the Word of the Lord is actually given the power to make their way successful.

> *Only be strong and very courageous, being careful to do according to all the law that Moses my servant commanded you. Do not turn from it to the right hand or to the left, that you may have good success wherever you go. This Book of the Law shall not depart from your mouth, but you shall meditate on it day and night, so that you may be careful to do according to all that is written in it. For then you will make your way prosperous, and **then you will have good success**. Have I not commanded you? Be strong and courageous. Do not be frightened,*

and do not be dismayed, for the LORD *your God is with you wherever you go.* (Joshua 1:7–9, emphasis mine)

Don't miss the principle of this passage. When you acknowledge and remain in Him, then YOU make your way prosperous. You activate the divine DNA of increase. Fruitfulness is normal for a healthy person. It is time to stop window shopping! God created you to be successful! It is time to unlock your divine DNA.

The third aspect is one that is oftentimes neglected. Remember, God's intention for us is not for mere spirituality but life in general and life as a whole. With this comes the reality that God intends for us to personally engage the laws of the Kingdom within our earthly sphere. God wants us to put things into action. It is easy for us to limit what God wants to do through us because we become passive with our faith. James expresses this nature of faith by stating that "faith without works is dead." Faith is not merely a philosophical exercise. Faith is never complete until it has done something. This is why we will not see increase in our life if we ONLY pray and do "spiritual things" with our faith. Faith, when coupled with action, becomes the hammer that breaks the window so we can access things on the other side!

It is critically important to realize that faith is something you have to use, or perhaps a better word is "employ." Perhaps you could say that faith is your employee. You put it to work in order to see God-sized things happen in your life. The writer of the book of James taught us that "faith without works is dead" (2:26 NKJV). Therefore, you have to take the unseen (and sometimes unfelt) evidence and do something with it. There are many different things we can put on faith's job description:

You can use faith to:

- Speak the Word of God when others says things that are negative or doubtful.
- Perform an act of kindness while serving someone who is less fortunate than you.
- Take a step toward your dream when others tell you to give up.
- Overcome mountains that have continually blocked your way to your destiny.

What is it that you could use faith for? How can you employ faith in your life? Let me remind you that God has already given you a measure of faith and that faith has the potential to make impossible things possible. As a believer, you are not bound to your past, stuck in your shame, or lost without direction. By faith, everything is now new. By faith, you are on the path to God's best. A great illustration of this principle of work can be found in one of the parables taught by Jesus—the parable of the talents.

A property owner goes on a long journey. In his absence, he puts his servants in charge of his possessions. To one of his workers, he gives five talents, which was a sum of money. To another worker, he gives two talents, and to a last servant he gives one. Upon his return from the journey, he checks with his workers to find out what they had done with his money. The one who had been given five made five more. The one who had been given two produced two more. But the last worker—out of fear—hid his talent in the ground and had done nothing to increase it. The last one was severely punished. Actually, the owner took the one talent and gave it to the one who had ten. Why? The owner expected increase.

The principle of work in the Kingdom is a key to release God's glory in the earth. God has given you everything that you need. Now it is your responsibility to work it. You have to make something out of what God has placed in your hand.

Remember Moses? He asked God how he could accomplish the task at hand. God's response to him was "What is in your hand?" In other words, use what you already have! Let me remind you there is a divine DNA inside you and that it has unlimited potential! You don't have to window shop anymore. It is time for you to step into your purpose and to fulfill your potential. This is your opportunity to see yourself as you really are. You were created for increase, and God has placed within you a divine capacity to be fruitful.

The next key that must be employed is the idea of sowing seeds. Sowing seeds is a principle that works automatically and regardless of whether we intend for it to work or not. The key to gaining increase in our life is to sow good seed beginning today. Sowing seed has three principles that must be honored:

1. The harvest you reap is directly connected to the seed you sow.
2. The amount of harvest you reap is proportionate to the amount of seed you sow.
3. The harvest is guaranteed as long as you do not give up.

Your fruitfulness is dependent upon you sowing seeds. It is important for you to know that the principle of reciprocity works for both good and bad seed. I want to encourage those of you have sown a lot of bad seed up to this point in your lives—don't get discouraged while you are replacing bad seed with good seed! As one preacher so aptly illustrated to me, you will still be harvesting the bad seeds while you are putting good seed in the ground[12]. "And let us not grow weary of doing good, for in due season you will reap IF you do not give up" (Galatians 6:9, emphasis mine). It may get frustrating at times when you are changing your life because you will still be reaping from a previous season. Don't quit! You were created to be fruitful and to increase. It is in your DNA. Begin today by employing the steps of increase. Acknowledge God. Remain in His Word, and work hard. Sow seeds. This is the guaranteed way to have everything that you need to fulfill purpose!

CHAPTER 8
YOUR DIVINE DNA: DOMINION
THE POSITION OF GLORY

Basketball is kind of like life—you can't score unless you have possession. One night I was sharing some skills with my daughter's basketball team regarding rebounding. My lesson focused on the importance of position when rebounding after a shot. I said, "Position gets possession." Position is everything when it comes to winning in life. Position can be defined in many different ways, and each of them have an impact on your posture in life. Position can be defined as the following:

1. "A place where someone or something is located or has been put
2. A particular way in which someone or something is placed or arranged

3. A situation or set of circumstances, especially one that affects one's power to act
4. A person's particular point of view or attitude toward something"[13]

These four definitions speak to four aspects of position that I want to address in this chapter—relocation, relationship, rulership, and representation. Each of these aspects of position influence what happens to you and what God can do through you.

First, *location* indicates the place where something or someone dwells. Your location is very important. Ask any realtor what one of the main determiners in market value is, and they will most likely answer, "Location, location, location." You have to position yourself to be "at the right place at the right time."

Relocation

Position is about location. Just as in sports, your position matters! Before Christ, your market share of spiritual real estate was terrible. The Bible called this a domain of darkness. Kind of sounds like something out of a horror flick, huh? Or at best one of the rides at Universal Studios. But this domain of darkness is to be feared much more than an expensive Hollywood film or a thrill-based amusement park ride. This domain of darkness holds people captive to things of the past. The terrain of terror infiltrates the mindsets of people made for greatness and tricks them into living lives of mediocrity. The domain of darkness hides the truth—truth right in front of you—the truth that offers a different path rather than one that leads to destruction. Men and women who are created to do great works find themselves enslaved by sin, fear, shame, and mindsets that rob them of life. To make it even more graphic, the Bible calls the offspring of this territory "children of wrath." There is no hope for us in this position.

However, as we have discovered, the Fall Guy made a way for us to be relocated. According to Colossians 1:13, "He has delivered us from the domain of darkness and transferred us to the kingdom of his beloved Son." This relocation grants you a new position in life. You are no longer enslaved to the "domain of darkness." You are no longer indebted to the judgment of sin. You are freed from the shame of yesterday. You have been relocated and given a new position to live life.

This new location has a different set of rules. You are now positioned in the Kingdom of God. The old domain had certain requirements and expectations of its citizens. Now you have been given rights and privileges of an entirely different territory. Learning these new rules will assist you in fulfilling the potential of your divine DNA. The problem I had was that even though I had been transferred into a new locale and was ruled by a different Sovereignty, I still had the same mindset and perspective on life.

The Elephant

Have you ever wondered how circuses can be deemed safe places when housed inside is one of earth's largest animals roaming around under a tent? It is fascinating when one discovers the process of taming these massive creatures. In order to tame these animals, zoo owners start when the elephants are young. As adult elephants, they have grown into the powerful creations that we observe, but as baby elephants, they are much more limited in strength. During this time of "powerlessness," the trainer binds them with chains strong enough to hold them. These chains, applied day in and day out, eventually shape the expectations and perspective of these elephants. Months later, after they have matured into full-grown beasts, their minds have already been conditioned into believing that they have no power over the restraint even though, as they have grown into adults, they have also grown in strength. They are "new" creatures now.

This is what happens to Christians. We spend our whole lives "trained" in the bondage of a sinful nature. Lusts, passions, fears, shame, defeats, etc., become a way of life. Later, after we accept Christ into our hearts, we find ourselves still living by the promptings of a mind that was trained as a child of wrath. Yes, our nature has changed, but our perspective has not.

Rulership

A second definition of position has to do with the stance or posture one takes as it relates to a viewpoint. The professor states, "My position on this is..." It is the perspective one takes in arguments, explanations, and theories. When you are born again, even your mindset is supposed to change. Paul communicates this transition when he states to the one who accepts Christ that old things pass away, and everything becomes new (See 2 Cor. 5:17). The Apostle Paul is not talking about tangible things like cars or clothing or houses. When I became a Christian, I didn't return to a new home after the service. When I professed Jesus as Lord, my clothes didn't magically become new. Paul is referring to your vantage point—your perspective on life. Your position changes. Rather than seeing yourself as a failure, you can see yourself as a victor. Rather than viewing life as a cup half empty, now you can see life as a cup overflowing. Your perspective changes as does your position to live life to the full. Isn't it time you embrace a new point of view? Isn't it time you step into the life God has already made available?

Relationship

A third aspect of position has to do with relationship. It is where you are "placed" in relation to God. As a believer, God has declared you righteous. God literally repositions your status. Before this supernatural change in your heart, you had no access to God, no relationship that granted you the privilege to be in His presence. But now, as a Christian, you are not just brought close as a friend; you are literally adopted into His family. You are a child of God. He relocates you. He changes your perspective, makes you more than a conqueror, and literally changes your status with Him.

You now have the same rights and privileges the Son of God did when He walked on the earth. Jesus came to restore to you that relationship as a child of God. Adam and Eve were not merely creatures. They were beings created in the image of God Himself. They were the progeny of the Creator. Remember, He created cows, which reproduces cows. He created lions to reproduce lions. And you were created to be like Him through this relationship of Father to children!

To unlock your divine DNA, it is necessary for you to recognize the work of relocation Christ did for you. After accepting Christ into your life, He moved you. He gave you a new location from which to do life.

Representation

Your relationship with God creates the responsibility for you to represent Him in the earth. This was God's original intent for humanity. In other words, man was created in God's image and God's likeness for *that* reason. God wanted man to be like Him on earth. Man was to be a mirror image of their creator. Unfortunately, sin scarred humanity so severely that this reflection was lost. Nevertheless, Christ came to restore our capacity to represent God. As children of God, "we are ambassadors for Christ, God making his appeal through us" (2 Corinthians 5:20). In no stretch of imagination, the Father expects for you and I to be like Him in the earth. Jesus came to show us how to live as humans. Too often, we excuse ourselves from the idea that we are supposed to be like Jesus. Nevertheless, Jesus showed up to show us how to show out for God. Jesus boldly said that we would do greater things than Him (See John 14:12). What is it that God is calling you to do? Get up tomorrow and go back to work with the mission of representing God to your boss, to your co-workers and to your friends. Change the atmosphere on behalf of the Father. Wherever you show up, show out for God.

Paul wrote, "For the creation waits with eager longing for the revealing of the sons of God" (Romans 8:19). Creation itself is waiting for your divine DNA to show up! It is time for you to embrace your true identity and realize what is in you has the capacity for rulership, relocation, relationship, and a call to representation. It is time to unlock your divine DNA and take YOUR position!

CHAPTER 9

YOUR DIVINE DNA: HEALTHY RELATIONSHIPS
THE DANCE OF GLORY

DNA can be defined as "the fundamental and distinctive characteristics or qualities of someone or something, especially when regarded as unchangeable."[14] The idea of DNA is that there are divine aspects innately woven into your being that create capacities and uniqueness. This fact has a two-fold reality that we must consider. First, your DNA is shaped in a unique way so that there is no one else who currently lives, who has lived, or who will ever live that is exactly like you. You are you. On the other hand, your DNA has, at the same time, connected you to the fact that you are human and made in the image of God. Thus, in order for you to truly live, you must learn your uniqueness as an individual but also your similarities to God (or at least your intended similarities). You were created by God, and His DNA is within you. As a result, you have the divine capacity and need for relationships.

You were divinely created to have healthy relationships. Your potential, purpose, and power in life are directly connected to the relationships in your life. You are meant to receive from, and give to, others. A relationship is that connection that involves a reciprocal relationship of giving and taking from other humans in your life. Interestingly, in the Garden, following most acts of creation, God would declare, "It is good." For every heavenly body, earthly formation, animal, and plant God declared it was good until He made the original man. For the first time, God said something wasn't good. He said, "It is not good for man to be alone."

God, more than anyone else, knows that we are created to be like Him. God understands this innately because of His own relationship in what we call the Trinity. The word trinity is not a biblical term but rather a term that describes a biblical reality. The trinity communicates that there are three persons existing together in the Godhead. You may know them as the Father, the Son, and the Holy Spirit. They exist together as the perfect example of unity in diversity. Each person of the Godhead exists with a different position, role, and responsibility, but each together form one entity—God. To be honest, that is about as far as I want to go on the theological discussion of this reality. To be even more honest, my finite being cannot wrap my mind around this reality. The only way I can come to terms with this is to have faith. I believe it is true because God is true.

You may say, "That is interesting, but what does this have to do with me?" You and I were created in the likeness of this God I just described. This means in order for you to be complete as a person, you have to be connected to other persons. There is no place for independence in the expression of true humanity. This is why one of the techniques that the enemy uses to destroy us is to separate us from each other. Sinfulness creates breaches in our relationships that cause loneliness, and Satan takes advantage of this loneliness, as illustrated in 1 Peter 5:8. Peter reveals a devious tactic as he says, "the enemy walks around like a roaring lion seeking whom he devour." According to one source, a lion is most successful when it hunts in darkness and in dense cover against an animal that is by itself.[15] The lion has the best opportunity to gain victory over its prey when that animal is alone. Your enemy understands this. Your enemy knows that if he can get you alone, or at least feeling alone, then he has his best chance to destroy you.

> The Father, the Son, and the Holy Spirit exist together as the perfect example of unity in diversity.

Healthy relationships fortify our lives as humans, and another tactic that the enemy uses is to get us to bite and devour one another (See Galatians 5:15). We need each other, but due to the brokenness within, we break what is around us. As you have heard it said, "Hurt people hurt people." Accordingly, we create defense strategies that cause us to disconnect from others. We believe this is what will keep us safe. If we are not close, then we won't be hurt, right? Unfortunately, this mode of thinking is shallow. Yes, being disconnected does keep us from being hurt initially, but the long-term effects of not connecting with people in healthy relationships are devastating. I will give you a strategy in a later chapter that outlines the steps that are necessary to restore broken relationships and will give you the empowerment to end toxic relationships.

Right now I want you to embrace a need in your life that, in some respects, our culture has taught us to avoid—relationships—by looking deeper into the way our Creator functions as unity in diversity. I like the way Catherine LaCugna describes this relationship of the trinity. She calls it a "divine dance."[16] Perhaps you have been dazzled by the artistic brilliance of the participants on the show *Dancing with the Stars*. There is something magical about watching two people seemingly glide through the air almost as if it they are not even touching the ground. The magic happens when two individuals are so synced together that they seem connected. Their movements complement each other and even seem to complete the other. This is the power of healthy relationships.

This is the type of synergy that is found in the trinity—God the Father, God the Son, and God the Holy Spirit in perfect unity, supporting the others, completing each other, and becoming something more than either could be by themselves. For us, our wholeness is dependent upon our vertical relationship with God Himself *and* our horizontal relationships with other people created in His image. John, also known as "the beloved," raises the standard on relationships with these words:

> *If someone says, 'I love God,' and hates his brother, he is a liar; for he who does not love his brother whom he has seen, how can he love God whom he has not seen?* (1 John 4:20 NKJV)

Did you catch this important reality? We cannot love God and hate our brother. This would be like me going up to someone and mistreating their child in front of them and then trying to pretend like I love them. I just hated on their kid, and now I want to buddy up with them. It doesn't work like that. Our being demands that we have healthy relationships in order to find our purpose and fulfill our potential. Life flows through relationships. Remember, God declares, "It is not good for man to be alone."

The Bible reveals the "divine dance" in operation even as Jesus was on the earth. The first glimpse of this relationship can be seen at the baptism of Jesus. The Holy Spirit's appearance in the form of a dove symbolizes support and affirmation, and then you hear the voice of the Father penetrate the earthly realm with these words: "This is my beloved Son in whom I am well pleased" (Matthew 3:17). Relationships are best when we sign up, show up, and speak up for those in our lives. Jesus signed up to serve. The Holy Spirit showed up to support. The Father spoke up to affirm. These three actions—signing up (commitment), showing up (loyalty), and speaking up (affirmation)—create an unstoppable force that nothing in all of heaven and Earth can conquer.

Imagine if we all did this for the people in our lives. Imagine what it would be like for you if you had people sign up, show up, and speak up for you. How much more could you accomplish? How differently would you approach life? You would have courage to do what you wouldn't have even tried before. Relationships—healthy relationships—cultivate human potential like no other force. Unity in diversity must not be underestimated.

Remember the Tower of Babel in Genesis 11? God chose to confuse their language in order to derail their efforts to build a name for themselves. Their pursuits were wrong, although their method was right. The enemy was a fast learner, and he now pursues to bankrupt the unity in marriages, partnerships, churches, and other institutions that are making a difference in the world. Relationships create capacity that no individual has in themselves alone.

Three Mandates for Relationships

In order for relationships to work properly in our lives, we must understand and honor three mandates for relationships. There is the priority of unity, the principle of servanthood, and the power of love. Recognizing the brokenness of the world in the which we live, we must take initiative to follow these mandates ourselves.

The Apostle Paul articulates these mandates for relationships in Philippians 2:

> *1 So if there is any encouragement in Christ, any comfort from love, any participation in the Spirit, any affection and sympathy, 2 complete my joy by being of the **same mind**, having the **same love**, being in full accord and of one mind. 3 Do nothing from selfish ambition or conceit, but in humility count others more significant than yourselves. 4 Let each of you look not only to his own interests, but also to the interests of others. Have this mind among yourselves, which is yours in Christ Jesus, 6 who, though he was in the form of God, did not count equality with God a thing to be grasped, 7 but emptied himself, **by taking the form of a servant**, being born in the likeness of men.* (Philippians 2:1-7, emphasis mine)

First, unity must be a priority that is embraced in order for relationships to become what they are meant to be. We have already discussed the power of unity. Jesus adds to this understanding when He declares that "if two of you agree on earth about anything they ask, it will be done..." (See Matthew 18:19). Unity creates possibilities. When we embrace this principle and commit to the priority of unity, many of the things that divide us in relationships lose their power. Winning the argument becomes less important than unity. Being "right" becomes less important than maintaining unity. Demanding our preferences becomes less important than protecting unity. Unity is the key to opening the door to experiences and opportunities that we are striving for with these other allegiances.

In order to walk in unity, it is important to recognize where disunity comes from. First of all, we must realize that our struggle is not with the other person. As we perceive relationships in light of the divine DNA, recognizing that all people are created in the image of God, then the way we approach everything changes (See 2 Corinthians 5:16). Now, we know that conflicts only come from two places. First, our struggle is with spirits that have been sent to rob God's glory and destroy man's purpose. It is the same strategy that we learned from the Fall. He questions God's Word in order for us to question God, and he questions our identity so we will question who we really are. He also questions the consequences of denying God and denying our true selves. These three goals of the enemy set us up for failure in life. Paul correctly states that our struggle is not with humans but with evil spirits. This understanding will assist us in becoming a partner with the other person rather than an enemy.

I learned a great strategy from a couple once who said that when they find themselves in an argument, they position themselves shoulder to shoulder, facing a couch, and direct their conversation toward the couch. With this method, the "emotional energy" that tends to elevate when we fight each other is diffused. The physical posture supports the spiritual reality that we are fighting together against an outside force.

The second reality that is a source of our disagreement is what happens within us. The biblical author James says it like this: "What causes quarrels and what causes fights among you? Is it not this, that your passions are at war within you?" (James 4:1). In this light, we see that the enemy is not the other person or even "the devil" but is actually ourselves. Too often we blame the enemy—"the devil made me do it"—when the truth be told, it was because of a battle we were losing on the inside of us that led to an external defeat.

The priority of unity is easier to maintain when we understand these two realities. The true enemy is a spirit that has already been defeated or a war within that we can take authority over. Too many wars (and relationships) are lost because we are fighting the wrong adversary the wrong way.

The second mandate that must be honored in relationships is the principle of servanthood. We learn this approach from the model of Jesus, who came to restore a relationship with you and me. Jesus came to serve, not to be served. This servant mentality opened the hearts of people to receive His truth—the truth that could set them free. That truth would restore them to the lost aspect of their healthy, divine DNA relationships. Notice in Philippians 2 that it says that Jesus "made" Himself a servant. In other words, this was an act of his will. He chose servanthood.

This is an important step to understand because Jesus had every right *not* to serve us. As the Son of God, He had the right to retain a position of glory and authority. Yet He "denied Himself" the privileges of deity in order to restore us to a right relationship. A right relationship was more important to Him than just maintaining a "right." In relationships, we have to deny ourselves in order to serve the relationship. Yes, we may have a right to do something different. Yes, it may not be easy, and most certainly, it may not be enjoyable at the moment. Yet the prize of relationship is worth the sacrifice of servanthood. Paul said it like this: "For though I am free from all, I have made myself a servant to all, that I might win more of them" (1 Corinthians 9:19). Servanthood is a key to the heart, which is the garden of relationships. But most of our relationships our like gardens overtaken with weeds because we haven't learned to serve.

The last mandate of relationships is the power of love. Most of the time we approach relationships by what we can get out of them. Incredibly, we do things for people so they will do something back for us. We learned this technique with the mantra "I will scratch your back IF you will scratch my back."

This subtle philosophy impacts the way we enter marriages, choose churches, and follow through with commitments. This contractual type of relationship is not based on love. Love is a covenant. Love is not love if it has to be reciprocated. Perhaps the best way to describe this concept is a term I learned from a professor. Dr. Wes challenged us to embrace an approach to relationships that he called "living from love." I had never heard this term before. It was a foreign language.

What does this mean? My relational context was based on living for love. I would do things to get things. I chose people because of what they could do for me. Living from love is not based on this give-and-take (and sometimes just "take") approach. Living from love is the foundational principle of Christianity. This is how the "divine dance" works. It is a posture in life and in relationships that creates a new paradigm for living. As my writing coach, Kary Oberbrunner, says often, we must "show up filled up" in our interactions with people.[17] Love is powerful because love doesn't need anything from others to make it work, but this concept is foreign to most people.

The scriptural basis for this principle can be found in multiple places in the Bible. First, let's look at 1 John 4:19. The author pens this principle as he writes, "We love because He first loved us." Our ability to love is based on the gracious act of God showing up filled up for us. He gave to us when we had nothing to give. He loved us when we hated Him. Living from love means you approach the relationship without needing anything because you are already full. This kind of love is God's kind of love. God doesn't *need* us to respond. He doesn't become less when we don't accept Him. No lack is created in Him when a human rejects Him. When we understand this concept, we can love people with authenticity, and their response doesn't challenge our identity. We show up, filled up in love, and this creates the environment where failure is not an option (See 1 Corinthians 13:1-8). Love never fails because the power of love is very practical. Paul writes this profound statement to the Corinthians in 2 Corinthians 5:

> *14 For the love of Christ controls us, because we have concluded this: that one has died for all, therefore all have died; 15 and he died for all, that those who live might no longer live for themselves but for him who for their sake died and was raised. 16 From now on, therefore, we regard no one according to the flesh.* (2 Corinthians 5:14-16)

We regard no one accordingly to the "flesh." When you begin to see people "through the spirit," the way God sees them, it will empower you to live from love. Remember, one of the components of divine DNA is healthy relationships. When you live from love, you are a healing agent in the lives of others. In this passage, we learn that the love of Christ controls us. This is the power of love. Love creates a capacity that you do not have in yourself. The word for control is quite revealing as it relates to how God's love controls us. The Greek word for control is *sunecho*. It can be translated in at least two ways: "to constrain" or "to compel"[18].

Love, then, gives you the power to be constrained, or to be compelled. First, the love of Christ constrains you from doing things you shouldn't do. In other words, when you want to slap that person that just "did stupid," the power of Christ's love within you holds you back. This is a good thing for relationships. Secondly, love compels you. This means that there is a force within you that gives you the power to do what you don't want to do. In other words, when you don't want to say, "I'm sorry," the love of Christ enables you to speak these words that are necessary to bring healing to the relationship.

These three mandates must be honored in order for relationships to work as God intended. You must prioritize unity over your personal wishes. You must submit to the principle of servanthood in order to open the hearts of those in your life for healthy connections. Lastly, you must utilize the power of love in order to operate in ways that, in and of yourself, are impossible. Nonetheless, the spirit of Christ within gives you the capacity to maintain unity, serve others, and walk in love.

Stewarding Your Relationships

Relationships don't just happen. There is the innate capacity that God places within us to have healthy relationships, yet we have a responsibility to steward the divine DNA of relationships. As each of the five components can thrive and fulfill their God-given purpose, each can also be squandered and lose their intended impact. There are three realities that must be considered when we are looking to steward our relationships.

First of all, the type of relationships that we have in our lives determines Earth's access to heaven. In other words, when we have relationships that are in right alignment, it creates an open door to God's presence. Vice versa, when we dishonor and abuse our earthly relationships, it impedes our heavenly relationship with God. There is no separation between vertical and horizontal relationships. These two aspects of relationship depend upon the other.

Jesus shows the significance of our earthly relationships and their impact in Matthew 5:21–26, where Jesus says, "If you are offering your gift and remember that your brother has something against you," stop what you are doing and go tend to that relationship first. Jesus is saying that a person cannot be right with Him if they are not right with their human counterparts. (Disclaimer: There are some relationships that just cannot work.) The Apostle Paul addresses this when he when he commands us to be at peace with everyone as much as it is up TO YOU (See Romans 12:18).

Secondly, the way we steward our relationships determines heaven's access to Earth. The writer John speaks to this in 1 John 4 when he creates a condition based on our willingness to love one another. He says,

"...if we love one another, God abides in us and His love is perfected in us" (1 John 4:12-13). The way we relate to each other has a direct impact on God's willingness to "abide" in our lives. This is clarified by stating that He remains with us by giving us His Spirit, and it is this Spirit of God that unlocks our divine DNA and restores to us the capacity to fulfill our God-given purpose. When we choose to dishonor and reject those people in our lives that are created in the image of God, we, in effect, reject the God who made them as well.

Lastly, the way we steward the relationships or, to say it another way, the way we treat people in our lives actually has an impact on our eternal status. That's right. The way we live and love here directly impacts our eternal existence. Let that sink in just a moment. The ramifications are huge. This should create a reason for each of us to examine our relationships and to commit to stewarding their place in our lives.

Our relationships on Earth reflect our relationships with God. We can be deceived into thinking that we have a good relationship with God while at the same time we hate on our spouses, our children, our co-workers, and unbelievers. People are not convinced of a God of love when His "people" express themselves in hate.

As you can see, our relationships have a profound impact on the "image" we present to the world. Relationships are intended to complete us, but too often when administered with a fallen mindset, relationships deplete us. God wants us to reflect Him in the earth. This includes the way we relate to each other.

God, teach us to dance the "divine dance"!

CHAPTER 10
YOUR DIVINE DNA: PURPOSE
THE WORK OF GLORY

A pen or a pencil may seem like an insignificant item. The average cost of a pencil, at the time of this writing, is around 15 cents. You can triple that cost for a pen. The pencil isn't that impressive. It is only around 7.5 inches long, and oftentimes it is an uninspiring yellow color. Yet we know that when a pencil (or a pen) is in the hands of the right person, in the right setting, and at the right time, significant, powerful (and sometimes miraculous) things can occur. Writing utensils can be used to create masterpieces—works of art that people travel the world over just to spend a view moments viewing from four feet away. A couple stands before a government official and signs paperwork that connects them together in a lifelong covenant called marriage. That same couple can then travel across town and sign another piece of paper committing to pay a half a million dollars over the next 30 years for their next home. A woman who is struggling to provide for her family could pick up a pencil and turn the words it writes into a bestseller, thereby creating an entirely new life for herself. Pencils and pens have a purpose: to express the desire, the imagination, and the intent of the person holding them.

Wrong Uses

It is very obvious what the purpose of a writing utensil is. Nevertheless, these tools don't always get used appropriately. Perhaps you have made the attempt to use a pencil to accomplish another task. You can attempt to dig holes with pencils, hammer things, or open boxes, and if you are a boy in elementary school, the pencil might become a mini weapon or a commanding sword! Either way, this object meant for one purpose can be used in other ways. As mentioned earlier, when something is used wrongly, there is the risk of damaging the object or the item on which the object is used. In other words, when purpose is abused, it creates brokenness.

You and I have a purpose. It is much more significant than waking up, going to work, coming home, going to sleep, and then repeating the cycle. You are a pencil in the hand of God. He has something to express through you, and you were created with a divine code. This divine code, when unlocked and released, becomes a powerful force that reflects God Himself in the earth. Your purpose is to be like God on the earth. Humanity was placed to run the earth just like God runs heaven.

In order to avoid forfeiting, abusing, and living below our potential, we must submit to our purpose.

I have created an acronym to help you recognize the "purpose of purpose" in your life.

P.U.R.P.O.S.E
Listed below are seven important aspects of purpose. Please take some time to think about your life and your purpose.

P–PRIORITY of purpose
U–UNIQUENESS of purpose
R–RESPONSIBILITIES of purpose
P–PLACE of purpose
O–OPPORTUNITY of purpose
S–3 S's of purpose
E–The EXTRA MILE of purpose

The PRIORITY of Purpose

First of all, the priority of purpose must be recognized. There is nothing in life more important than fulfilling your purpose, but this can only be understood when you consider a couple of important points. God created you, and God does nothing accidentally or without reason. As we have already highlighted, you were fearfully and wonderfully made. He took time to think about you, your gifts, your passions, and your personality. Everything was thought out and thought through. Your divine DNA is strategically placed within you ON PURPOSE FOR A PURPOSE! When we submit our lives to this purpose, we become aligned with heavenly intention, and this is a powerful place to live. If we were to look at the Scriptures, we can see the Bible calling us to live according to the priority of our purpose.

> *So, whether you eat or drink, or whatever you do, do all to the glory of God.* (1 Corinthians 10:31)

> *30 He must increase, but I must decrease. 31 He who comes from above is above all. He who is of the earth belongs to the earth and speaks in an earthly way. He who comes from heaven is above all.* (John 3:30–31)

Once we learn to approach life on purpose with His purpose as our priority, everything takes on a new meaning. We learn that this life is not all there is. In essence, this life is only preparation for true life, eternal life. Some may say this kind of talk takes the fun out of life. That's religion. I am talking about an intimate love relationship with a God who cares enough for us to direct our steps. The wonderful thing about the place where He is taking us is that He is already there. He is inviting us to enter the future, that place He has already prepared for us.

The UNIQUENESS of Purpose

A second aspect of purpose that you must understand is the reality that no one else has your specific calling. You are unique. There is no one, in all of history, who has the exact gift-mix, personality, and experiences that were combined together to make you into you! The psalmist pens some beautiful words that express this amazing truth. Read this passage and embrace the truth about you:

> *For you formed my inward parts; you knitted me together in my mother's womb. I praise you, for I am fearfully and wonderfully made. Wonderful are your works; my souls knows it very well. My frame was not hidden from you,*

when I was being made in secret, intricately woven in the depths of the earth. (Psalm 139:13–15)

Do you see the words selected for this passage? "You formed me"; "I am fearfully and wonderfully made" and "intricately woven." The author then reveals another truth about you. God doesn't make mistakes. He doesn't make average things; His works are wonderful. You are a wonderful masterpiece of a Divine Being who has no limits. You are fearfully and wonderfully made by a God who does wonderful things. There is nothing insignificant about you! Go ahead and say it: "There is nothing insignificant about me!" Okay, say it again. This is a part of your unlocking the divine DNA within you.

The treasure of you is already there. God has already deposited it within you. You could say that you were God's vault, and your task is to discover the code that unlocks your life's potential! No one else can be you. No one else is meant to be you. You and your purpose are unique. Paul addresses this as well when he writes about the complexity of the Church. We are "one body" but many parts (See 1 Corinthians 12:12). When you begin to understand that you have been created, chosen, and commissioned by God for a unique purpose and for this particular time in history, you will begin to step into your divine destiny.

Paul declares that we have different gifts according to the grace that God gives us. When you discover the unique mix of your gifts and then embrace your calling, it positions you to live life to the full. It also creates boundaries that your enemies cannot cross. God will see to it that a person rightfully aligned, utilizing their gifts, and fulfilling their purpose is protected by heaven itself. This is a powerful place to live.

The RESPONSIBILITIES of Purpose

Once we embrace the priority and the uniqueness of our purpose, we feel the burden to fulfill our responsibilities of purpose. Valuables and significant resources must be properly stewarded. When we understand how valuable and significant we are, it is easier to understand why God calls us to steward our lives appropriately.

I recently upgraded my wife's wedding ring. The cost was significantly more than the original ring that I bought for her over 20 years ago. As a result of the value of this ring, we have chosen to insure it in order to protect it. It's value created a new responsibility. In the same way, your life has a purpose that must be stewarded. It is connected to your divine DNA and the will of God for your life. Because of this, Paul tells us to walk worthy of our calling (See Ephesians 4:1-6). There are different aspects to being responsible for our purpose and walking worthy of our calling.

The Apostle Paul reveals his strategy to walk worthy in 1 Corinthians 9. He talks about his relationships with others and the priority he places on serving them in order to win them to Christ. Secondly, we are to run the race to win. Do we often get satisfied with just being in the game? The heartbeat of God for you is that you achieve greatness. You were created to rule and to increase. This must be remembered as you are thinking about your purpose. Have you set the bar too low? Are you settling for second best?

In order to be ready to shine, we must be equipped. In order to achieve our best, we must be disciplined. Interestingly, the Apostle connects the way he prepares his body to his spiritual capacity. As a matter of fact, Paul says these exact words: "…I discipline my body and keep it under control, lest after preaching to others I myself should be disqualified" (1 Corinthians 9:27). This is really an amazing statement. The way he lived physically directly impacted his spiritual qualification. We addressed this earlier when we talked about our being as the combination of a body, soul, and spirit. These components are woven together with such sophistication that they cannot be divided into separate categories. When you are tired physically, it affects you emotionally. When you are distracted emotionally, it impacts you spiritually. We must be responsible with our whole being in order to achieve our full potential.

It would be nice if God could just "zap" us and miraculously make everything work. The reality of this journey is that we have to partner with God's work. We must work out as He works in us. If we want greatness, it requires us to be good stewards of our purpose. One of my best friends, Jeff Timbs, had a favorite verse that spoke to this fact: "Where there are no oxen, the manger is clean, but abundant crops come by the strength of the ox" (Proverbs 14:4). In other words, if you want the strength of the ox, you have to put up with its crap. Greatness comes with a price.

The PLACE of purpose

In Acts 17:26, we discover that "he made from one man every nation of mankind to live on all the face of the earth, having determined allotted periods and the boundaries of their dwelling place." In other words, God has determined "a place" for you to fulfill your purpose in the earth. You are not here by accident. God has given you a specific and certain domain to rule.

In the same way that God placed Adam in the Garden with the assignment to tend and to keep it, He has given you a certain place to live life. Before you were born, the Divine Designer crafted you with gifts and inherent skills. Then, he looked at the earth and drew an "X" and said, "Go and steward that place on the earth." Your place may include a geographic location, or it also may be a group of people or a particular career. Once you embrace this "place", you will find the sweet spot for your potential.

The OPPORTUNITY of Purpose

One of the things that we need to understand about purpose is that it is time sensitive. God was so intentional about your existence that He determined when you would exist. He literally decided that you would be alive in this time and this age. You are not the result of chance or a mere spontaneous result of some meteoric collision. God decided the intricate details of how you would be framed as well as when you would dwell on the earth. Thus, you can say you are perfectly fitted for "such a time as this" (See Esther 4:14). Also, the psalmist reveals that God thoughtfully wrote a journal of your future (See Psalm 139:16). Each and every day of your life has been penned by God. There are some keys that help you honor this time-stamp on your purpose.

There is importance in "counting the days." In other words, you should live life on purpose. Each day counts, and so you count each day. Another psalm reveals the significance of counting our days. Psalm 90:12 reads,

"So teach us to number our days that we may gain a heart of wisdom." The psalmist reveals a secret for us to walk with wisdom in our lives. He says that as we learn to "number" or count our days, our hearts receive the capacity to have wisdom. Wisdom is not just knowledge. All of us have knowledge. You have heard it said that "knowledge is power." This is not exactly true. One can have knowledge and be powerless if they don't know how to use the knowledge or simply choose not to use the knowledge. Wisdom is the ability to know what to do with knowledge. This is power. Counting the days aligns our hearts with divine purpose. It calls the faculties of our being into order with what God has called us to do. When we have organized our lives according to time, we are empowered to make better choices and to live more effective lives.

This time-stamp understanding helps us realize that our lives on Earth are not immortal. It creates a soberness to the way we spend each day. Why? We will be held accountable with what we do with them. You could say that each day is a gift that God has given us to fulfill our purposes. He has allotted to each of us a number of days in order that His intentions for us should be fulfilled. With this allotment of days, He has determined an expiration date. Hebrews 9:27 says, "…it is appointed for man to die once, and after that comes judgment." Each of us are going to die.

But that's not the main point. The main point is that each of us are going to be held accountable for how we lived. Your life is a test. Learning to number your days helps you to order your life with intentionality that aligns with your divine purpose. You have an opportunity to fulfill purpose.

Lastly, a positive goal for you to embrace is that God is preparing to reward you for your performance. I know we have spent a lot of energy on the fact that our salvation is not based on works. This is perfectly accurate. But what we have missed is the reality that getting saved and fulfilling purpose are two different things. You can be saved and miss your purpose. I want you to fulfill your purpose. I want you to succeed at the opportunity of purpose.

The 3 S's of Purpose

The next letter in our acronym is S. This letter expresses three important aspects of purpose that help us further. When we walk in our purpose, we have the blessing of a divine shield, the provision of satisfaction, and a glorious shine on our lives. These three components—the shield, the satisfaction, and the shine—cultivate a life that is incomparable. When a person is truly fulfilling their purpose, it is an amazing place to be. It is what Jesus called "life to the full."

Divine Shield

First of all, when you are walking according to purpose, there is a *divine shield* that is assigned to your life to protect you from the enemy. Paul declares that everything works together for good for those who love God *and* are called according to His purpose (See Romans 8:28). In other words, God is personally involved in working out the details of your journey when you are living for His glory. He wants you to succeed. He wants you to be victorious. Why? You are representing Him. You are

His reflection in the earth. If your life is characterized by failure, loss, lack, and defeat, this does nothing for Him, His glory, or expanding His Kingdom.

This same protection of purpose that we should expect in our lives was at work in the life of Jesus. In Luke 4, some of the religious leaders had had enough of this Nazarene. Filled with violent anger, they plotted to apprehend Jesus and throw him over a cliff. The plan was placed in motion. These confused, passionate religious leaders caught Jesus and forced him outside the city, where they intended to end His life. Surprisingly, the Scriptures reveal a turn in the story. Jesus simply walked away from the danger right through the middle of His enemies (See Luke 4:28-32). He was outnumbered. There was no physical possibility for Him to escape. They had already proven that they could overpower Him and force him outside of town. This is where the shield of purpose comes in. His purpose had not been completed. His purpose, in effect, overpowered their evil intentions.

Another story I am reminded of took place in Babylon thousands of years ago. A man named Daniel, who had established himself as a man of God, a man of faith, became the center of an evil storm. His contemporaries realized that Daniel lived such an excellent life that the only thing that they could do would be to create an issue around his faith. Thus, they devised a plan for his destruction. King Darius was in power at this time, ruling over the Babylonian kingdom. He had appointed 120 chief administrators to rule throughout his domain. He then placed three officers over the 120. But Daniel was promoted above all 123 of these men. He lived and led in such a way that even as a foreigner, he was promoted in the ranks. The others, filled with jealousy and hatred, invented a way to remove him from his position. As a matter of fact, his enemies didn't just want to remove him from his position; they wanted to take away his life. Look at this statement concerning Daniel's life:

> *4 Then the high officials and the satraps sought to find a ground for complaint against Daniel with regard to the kingdom, but they could find no ground for complaint or any fault, because he was faithful, and no error or fault was found in him. 5 Then these men said, "We shall not find any ground for complaint against this Daniel unless we find it in connection with the law of his God."* (Daniel 6:4–5)

The only place they could find to accuse Daniel was in connection to his relationship with God. Thus, these resentful men approached the king with shallow flattery and suggested a new law. This law stated that no one could pray to any god except King Darius for a period of 30 days. Kings, of course, were seen to be infallible. Thus, it wasn't a great stretch for King Darius to impose such a decree, especially for just 30 days. The problem was that Daniel had a custom of praying three times each day. For these green-eyed men, this was 90 opportunities to take Daniel out.

As the story goes, King Darius signed the law into existence, and the 120 waited for Daniel to pray. Of course, right on time, Daniel approached the presence of God through prayer. The first priority of our purpose is always our love relationship with God. Out of this relationship our activities flow. As someone said once,

"Out of being flows our doing." As soon as Daniel began his prayers, the men ran to the king and exposed Daniel. If you grew up in Sunday School, you know this story as "Daniel and the Lions' Den." King Darius, who sincerely liked Daniel, regretted his selfish decree. Nevertheless, in order to protect his kingship, he had to go through with his mandate. King Darius commanded for Daniel to be thrown into the lions' den as punishment for his defiance to this new law. Nevertheless, Daniel's purpose had not been expended, and accordingly, the "divine shield" was in place. God responded to the king's command with a greater command. He charged an angel to govern Daniel's sleep (and perhaps even to cover the mouths of the lions). While Daniel slept like a baby, the king tossed and turned as he waited to see the outcome of what would be one of his most regretful acts as king.

As the first light of the sun touched the earth, the king hurriedly went to the lions' den. Once he was close enough, he cried out to his friend and trusted officer: "Daniel, was God able to save you?" And of course, with the divine shield in place, this man of God replied, "My God sent His angel to protect me!"

What is awesome is that God didn't have to come Himself. He sent, according to Daniel, only one angel. One angel is all it took to overthrow the king's command and the hunger of the lions. The lions were no doubt hungry, because as the story continues, King Darius commanded for Daniel's accusers to meet the same judgment. The Bible says that *before* these people had reached the bottom of the den, the lions "broke all their bones in pieces." The only explanation was a divine shield! When a person is fulfilling their purpose, nothing can threaten them.

Divine Satisfaction

The next S is satisfaction. There is nothing more satisfying then fulfilling your purpose. Once you have identified your divine DNA and unlocked it, your life goes to a whole other level. Every day becomes a fulfillment of God's journal for your life. You are living the very reason why you were created, and there is something special—no, supernatural—about this kind of life.

This divine satisfaction can be seen in the life of Jesus Christ on a trip through Samaria. As a reader, one can find a sense of urgency, or intentionality, as He directs His journey through Samaria. The Bible says in John 4:4, "He had to pass through Samaria." It is believed that the Jews avoided Samaria because of the tensions they had with Samaritans.[19] Jesus was following the will of His father. He was there on purpose. Let's look at the interchange between Jesus and His disciples after the woman had returned home rather than on the story itself.

The disciples were amazed that He was talking to a woman (cultural rule broken). But rather than bringing this supposed faux pas to His attention, they pushed the conversation to food. They encouraged the Rabbi to eat something. Perhaps they thought this was why they had been sent to town. I wonder if Jesus had sent them away in order to have this conversation with the woman, not out of impurity but for the purpose of creating a moment of authenticity for He and the woman to have a truth talk. This was no doubt exhilarating and fulfilling to Jesus. Speaking truth into the lives of people is why He was sent to the earth. He came to set people free from sins, from hopelessness, and from brokenness. He reveals how this happens in another one of His conversations: "…you will know the truth, and the truth will set you free" (John 8:32). His mission was to be the truth and speak the truth into people because this was the key to their salvation, their freedom. Doing this, being this, was His purpose. And doing this, being this, satisfied Him more than anything else.

His response to the disciples after their prompting to eat expresses this principle of divine satisfaction when we walk in our purpose. He said, "My food is to do the will of Him who sent me and to accomplish His work" (John 4:34). How about you? What satisfies? What is more important than food to you? What fulfills you more than your daily bread? Whatever that is, that is your purpose. When you find that and fulfill it, you will begin to experience life and life to the full. God doesn't just want you healed. He has commissioned you to heal others. He doesn't just want you blessed. He blesses you to bless others. This principle can also be found in another saying of Jesus: "…It is more blessed to give than to receive" (Acts 20:35).

When you unlock your divine DNA, you will become a powerful conduit where heavenly power flows through you to others. Stop and think about that just for moment. **God wants to extend Himself into the earth through you**. He wants to heal people through you. He wants to deliver people through you. He wants to provide for people through you. Your purpose is to image God in the earth. The key to fulfilling your purpose is to unlock the divine DNA so that you can discover the place of blessing, increase, dominion, and healthy relationship along with the expansion of God's Kingdom into your earthly domain. This is your purpose! When you find it and walk in it, you will be divinely satisfied!

The Divine Shine

When you begin to understand that God is protecting you and that God is using you, a glory begins to rest on your life that cannot be contained. Your life begins to exhibit a luster that before was hidden behind the shadows of shame and confusion. A life of fulfilled purpose creates a glow that is apparent. Maybe that's why we are called a "light that cannot be hidden" (See Matthew 5:14 NIV). This divine shine is automatic for those who are authentic and whole in who they are *and* what they are doing. A true synergy of a person in being and doing produces a glorious reflection of God Himself. This is the imago Dei. This is you being like God.

A person who discovers their purpose begins to walk out the original intention that God has for humanity. Your purpose is to shine with glory. This is the glory that humanity lost as a result of sin (See Romans 3:23). You were created to shine!

> *Fear not, for I am with you; I will bring your offspring from the east, and from the west I will gather you. ...Do not withhold; bring my sons from afar and my daughters from the end of the earth, everyone who is called by my name, whom I created for my glory, whom I formed and made.* (Isaiah 43:5–7)

The prophet reveals just how special you are. I encourage you to not underestimate the divine DNA that is deposited inside you. I want you to go on this journey, unlocking your full potential. As a matter of fact, you were created to express glory in your life. Go ahead and examine yourself. Is your life glorious? Are you satisfied? Are you walking with protection? Are you shining? You were formed within the mind of God and made within the womb of your mother to be birthed into the earth as a reflection of God Himself. Isn't it amazing the anticipation, the expectation, that God has for you? With all of our hang-ups, our failures, and our disappointments, this idea of being like God seems so improbable. Really, it's unfathomable that you and I could aspire to such lofty goals. To be honest, it would be impossible if God Himself had not fearfully and wonderful made you. It would be completely ludicrous except that right now, inside you, is God's DNA. A part of God is in you.

We could ask the question "What was God thinking?" What does He have in mind to invest a part of Himself inside us? The Apostle Paul gives us a glimpse into this glorious intent in Ephesians 3.

> *9 and to bring to light for everyone what is the plan of the mystery hidden for ages in God who created all things, 10 so that through the church the manifold wisdom of God might now be made known to the rulers and authorities in the heavenly places. 11 This was according to the eternal purpose that he has realized in Christ Jesus our Lord...* (Ephesians 3:9-11)

Paul speaks to this mystery. He declares God has chosen you to reveal His wisdom. Amazingly, it is not solely to the world that God wants to demonstrate His wise capacities. You and I are created to show rulers and authorities in heavenly places how wise God is. Wow! We should think about that for a moment when we find ourselves overwhelmed with the details of our earthly journey—mowing yards, changing diapers, cleaning up spilled milk, and chasing the dog after a storm. These things keep us busy with temporal pursuits, and all the while, there are principalities and powers peering through another dimension observing us, seeing us from the unseen world. Perhaps God has a conversation with them like He did with the devil about Job. "Have you consider my servant _____?" Go ahead—put your name there. The fact is that God has big plans for you. He has created you for big things. You are created for God's glory. You are created to shine with an inextinguishable light. This is why Jesus describes us with the same title as He had. He said, "you are the light of the world", a city on a hill that cannot be hidden (see Matthew 5:14).

You see, when you begin to walk in your blessings, continually increase in your potential, step into your position of ruling, and cultivate healthy relationships that are expressive of divine unity, you will finally fulfill the unique, divine purpose you were called to, and you will be an explosion of testimony for God. You are like a lightning bolt that lights up the sky on a dark summer night. You are His star. You are His glory. Isn't it time for you to embrace your divine shine?

The EXTRA MILE of Purpose

The last letter in this acronym for purpose is E. It articulates the idea of going the extra mile. This has to with the posture that we must embrace in life in order to excel, in order to shine. Paul charges us to walk worthy of the calling that we have received from God (See

Ephesians 4:1). To the Colossians, he declares that whatever we do, we should do it with all of our hearts.

23 Whatever you do, work heartily, as for the Lord and not for men, 24 knowing that from the Lord you will receive the inheritance as your reward. You are serving the Lord Christ. (Colossians 3:23–24)

Paul doesn't limit our pursuits to merely "spiritual activities." He removes the categories that we create for being "Christian." We have this ability to separate our church experiences from other experiences. We give ourselves to worship services, not realizing that God has made us to express glory in every venture of humanity. In another place, Paul echoes this idea by saying, "So, whether you eat or drink, or whatever you do, do all to the glory of God" (1 Corinthians 10:31). This really changes the way we do life. This means that when you are at the Mexican restaurant, let the way you are going about eating bring glory to God. When you are playing football on a Saturday afternoon, your tackle should bring glory to God. Everything should reflect His image in the earth. He created you to be blessed, to increase, to rule. He created you to do this in a way that fosters healthy relationships and serves your divine purpose. When you embrace this mindset, then you realize that "the finish line" is really only the halfway mark. Jesus said it like this: "If anyone forces you to go one mile, go with him two miles" (Matthew 5:41). When we learn to dig within ourselves, into the place where our divine DNA is locked up, we realize that our humanity was created to be and to do much more than we have given ourselves credit for. There is no such thing as "only human" when humanity is like God.

PART THREE

ENTERING YOUR FUTURE

CHAPTER 11
THE DIVINE TRANSFER
ON EARTH AS IT IS IN HEAVEN

> "I am not afraid of what my future holds,
> I am embracing it."
>
> —Aria Tweedy[20]

As we transition into the final section of our book, my aim is to give you the tools to enter your future. I know that phrase seems a little odd, because how can someone "enter the future"? Let me remind you that God has already intentionally, strategically determined His will for your life. What God has prepared for you…already is. The psalmist reveals to us the existence of a divine journal, where God Himself has written notes about each and every day you would spend on this earth. The future of your life was already written before your past was lived. The key then is to learn how to allow the words of God about you to determine your next steps rather than the scripts of your past. In other words, which book are you getting your instructions from? Are you living from the scripts of your past or the promise book of your future?[21]

The five components of your divine DNA already exist: your blessings, your fruitfulness, your dominion, your healthy relationships, and your purpose already exist! It is *your* divine DNA. And yet the realization of it waits to be unlocked. I don't want you to miss the life God has for you. As a result of sin, fear, disbelief, and confusion, we live out an existence that is far below God's glorious intention for us. We embrace an identity based on our past and find ourselves enslaved in a present reality that contradicts and even competes with our intended purpose. In this final section, I will share with you principles, methods, and tools that will empower you to enter the future, the reality that God has already determined for you.

You must understand that this divine transfer involves a combination of grace, human effort, and time. Grace is God's heavenly resources, human effort is our partnership with God, and time is the necessary commodity that we need to prepare ourselves to steward God's resources. It doesn't happen overnight. My childhood pastor, Gerald McGinnis, illustrated this principle with a coke bottle. You can spend hours and perhaps days meticulously forcing a wire into a soda bottle, and the wire inevitably takes on the shape of the bottle. The wire sits constrained and forced to stay within the boundaries set for it. One way to free the wire would be to smash the glass bottle that holds it. At that moment, the glass breaks, and the wire is freed. Nevertheless, it still retains the shape of the bottle. This is similar to what happens to us. Jesus smashes sin and bondage off our lives but we are still "wired" the same. Unlocking your divine DNA involves a process of partnering with God's grace and committing to a life of transformation.

You will need miraculous power along the way because there are strongholds in your life that have been strategically formed by the work of your enemy. God's foe (which by default is your enemy) doesn't want you to discover the keys to unlocking your divine DNA. His goal is to cause you to miss a relationship with God completely and, at the very least, go through life as a Christian but never truly stepping into your divine purpose. On the other hand, God sends aid to you through ministering angels, the manifestation of spiritual gifts and grace. Nevertheless, it is important to realize that this is not enough. If it was only up to God and His work, then all of us, all of humanity, would be conformed into the image of God and never walk in failure. On the contrary, God established human existence on the earth to very much be responsible for how life plays out. He created man to cooperate with His heavenly principles in the earthly realm. The key to unlocking purpose has to do with you honoring and mandating the heavenly laws.

Therefore, it is necessary for you and me to learn how to use the "keys of the kingdom" to unlock the divine resources. It is up to us to submit to God's power and welcome it into our lives. You may say, "It is not up to me. 'It is not of works lest any man should boast'"(See Ephesians 2:9). This is correct as it relates to salvation. You can't smash the bottle. Jesus did that. There is nothing that you can do in and of yourself that brings you into a relationship with Jesus Christ. Jesus is the door.

Once you accept Jesus, you receive everything you need to reclaim your rightful identity.[22] Entering your future happens after you start allowing the work of salvation to redefine your world. Jesus worked His salvation *in* you. It is your responsibility to work *out* His salvation. In other words, Jesus got heaven in you, and it is your job to get heaven in the earth. Paul reveals this principle in 2 Corinthians 6:1 when he says *to believers* to "not receive the grace of God in vain." Don't be one of those who receive grace and then somehow forfeit its work in their life.

Unfortunately, many people make eternity and miss heaven on earth. They will go through life and ultimately stand before God having never truly been transformed into the image of God in accordance with His original intent. I have written this book so that you will not be like that. These keys will help you unlock your Divine DNA and become who you were created to be. As an additional resource, consider joining a group of people walking this same journey out with a coach who creates more opportunities for you to be transformed. For more information, visit our website at www.tonycolson.com.

The Six Circles

To understand how this transformation in your life works, I want to introduce you to the six circles. Each of these circles has a profound impact on your life. I want to show you how to make these circles work for you. These circles include the body, the soul, the domain of darkness, the Kingdom, the world, and the spirit realm. We have already talked about the role of God in your life. He takes the initiative and invites you into a relationship with Him. This relationship begins within your spirit. Before you accept Christ, your spirit is dead. The Bible actually calls this condition before Christ as being "dead in sins." You function out of your soul and body. Before Christ, the spirit, where your divine DNA dwells, is locked up in a chamber of death.

Miraculously, something profound happens to a person when they accept Jesus as Lord. Their spirit is made alive by God's Spirit, who enters the person's spirit, and instantly, supernaturally, they are "born again." This is what the Bible calls a new creation. A person is a new creation because *before Christ*, their reality was strictly existing as a soul and body. The spirit was dead. In Christ, we are opened up to a whole new reality.

All of us are very familiar with life through the lens of our souls and bodies. I don't need to write about that. In essence, this is our problem. This is your problem. We are comfortably confined to living life solely from the vantage point of our souls and bodies. Even after we accept Jesus and our spirits are made alive, by default, we still function out of the soul and body. We must learn to "walk by the spirit" and not "the flesh." The flesh is that part of you that is driven by either the soul or the body.

The Body

The body is that part of our being that is in direct contact with the earthly realm. Our bodies can sense the elements of our surroundings. We feel when it is hot or cold outside. We are aware when raindrops are falling on our heads. Our bodies are also impacted by how we use them. When we do not get enough sleep or if we overexert our bodies, we feel tired or exhausted. We may become winded or our muscles may ache. The body is one of the circles that has a profound influence on us.

The Soul

Another circle that impacts the way we live is the soul. The soul is comprised of three aspects—the mind, the will, and the emotions. This trait of humanity can be comprehended better as we understand we were created in the likeness of God. He also is comprised of three aspects—the Father, the Son, and the Holy Spirit. Every human being is born in touch with this part of their being. Babies begin with thoughts, desires, and feelings even within the womb. If a baby is hungry, it will signal its body to scream out of anger—anger that the mother or father will quickly respond to.

As an infant, this expression of the mind, the will, and the emotions is attached mostly to basic human need. Over time, however, our souls begin to make interpretations of their inward feelings and the encounters the body has with the world. These interpretations ultimately form into systems of thought and belief. As these systems are affirmed and used over and over again, they become scripts that play out almost automatically. Eventually, things that happen to us, actions by others, smells, and even feelings that rise up initiate a pattern of behavior that we follow blindly as if we are no longer in control.

The World

Another circle is the world—the earthly realm that is made up of physical components. It is the dimension that we can see, smell, feel, and taste. It is this realm that must be respected and understood. The world was created to be the domain of rule for mankind, and we were sent here as ambassadors of God Himself. In other words, mankind is supposed to represent the Creator to the earth. Unfortunately, sin caused mankind to forfeit this position.

As Pastor Ron Carpenter teaches, this world was created to be governed by Kingdom principles[23]. Sadly, the world is no longer under the rule of righteousness. Creation itself is waiting on you to unlock your divine DNA.

> *For the creation waits with eager longing for the revealing of the sons of God.* (Romans 8:19)

Wait! Stop. Think about that. Creation is waiting on you! You have to use the keys to unlock your divine DNA. You were created for this purpose. The world is waiting on you to show up. Your family needs you. Life needs you to step into your created purpose!

The Domain of Darkness

There is another influence at work in our lives called the domain of darkness. This realm houses spirits, principalities, and powers that are unseen. Yet though they are invisible, they are at work to destroy us. These spirits of darkness have access, in some mysterious way, to our minds. They speak ideas and thoughts into our minds, which we must interpret. It is my belief that these spirits are assigned to you at birth and strive to influence your life in a way that leads you away from your true identity. They want you to embrace a lie, and they want to hide the truth from you. They want to cause you to believe things about yourself and God that are not true. These spirits operate in the same posture as the serpent, who stealthily deceived Eve and tripped up Adam. You are an offspring of Adam and therefore their target. More importantly, you are a creation of God who was created to be His image in the earth, so they feverishly work to keep you locked up in the prison of self-deception. These dark forces are the reason that as early as you can remember, you had a propensity toward certain things. Satan is not omnipresent like God, and therefore certain spirits are assigned to each individual in the same way that God appoints angels as "ministering spirits" for His children. (See Hebrews 1:14.) Some individuals may be targeted by a spirit of lust, while others are attacked by greed, malice, or lying. These spirits strategically work in such a way that they can cause a person to embrace a certain identity based on these lies. The reality is that each of us was born with the capacity to follow any course—from the greatest of pursuits to the most unimaginable evils.

The mind, will, and emotions make decisions based on their interpretation of thoughts, desires, and feelings. Without God, the soul's context is limited to its past experiences and its present understanding. Thus, the soul can greatly misunderstand reality. What if your current reality is based on lies? What if you are not destined to be like your father? What if there is another set of lenses available where you can see a different course of life?

The Kingdom of God

This is the advantage of a person who accepts Jesus Christ. They are awakened to a whole new reality. You, as a believer, are given access to God Himself, and God places His Spirit within you to be with you at all times. As you learn to rely on this new relationship with God, you become empowered to unlock your divine DNA and begin to walk in your blessings, fruitfulness, dominion, healthy relationships, and purpose as you were intended to. This relationship changes everything! It is God's intention that His Kingdom establishes His rule in your life. The Kingdom of God is always available to inform and to reorder your earthly realm. Again, this is why Jesus taught His disciples to pray in this way: "Your Kingdom come , your will be done on earth as it is in Heaven" (Matthew 6:10). This is the will of the Father. He wants the Kingdom to become the primary expression within your reality. The Kingdom is a kingdom of light and therefore always has authority over any other realm. As you learn the keys to the kingdom, it will unlock this reality. This has to be initiated in the spirit.

Your Spirit

The spirit realm is the final circle. Your spirit has the opportunity to see things differently. The door swings opens when your divine DNA is activated through faith, and once you learn to live by the spirit, everything changes. The advantage is that now you have access to God's Spirit in your spirit. In a very real sense, you have complete access to God Himself. This spirit to Spirit relationship positions you to reclaim the glory that was lost on your life. Thus, the goal is for your life to be primarily ordered by the Spirit in the spirit! The technique that I am about to teach you will assist in bringing your body and soul into alignment with the spirit. When this happens, nothing is impossible.

Remember, the spirit is what has direct access to God Himself. Therefore, your aim should be to surrender your spirit, soul, and body to the one who fearfully and wonderfully made you. The aim is to allow God, the one who has written your best days in His book, to show you the way to increase from glory to glory. He is for you and not against you. He has a plan that involves a future and a hope. Are you ready to unlock the future and make it a reality? Let's go visit "The Mirror"!

CHAPTER 12
THE MIRROR MINDSET
DON'T FORGET WHO YOU REALLY ARE

> "But we all, with unveiled face, beholding as in a mirror the glory of the Lord, are being transformed into the same image from glory to glory, just as by the Spirit of the Lord."
>
> —2 Corinthians 3:18 NKJV

The Mirror

Mirrors reflect images. It really isn't a difficult concept. You look in the mirror to see what you look like. In the passage above, we learn that we can see "glory" when we look into something that is similar to a mirror. The question is, "What is the mirror?" Where can we find this divine tool in order to see what God wants us to be like? But not to just see what God wants us to be like—once we look at it, it then gives us the power to become it. Could you imagine the demand for such a mirror? Ladies would rush to the store to buy a mirror that guaranteed that after looking in it their wrinkles would be tightened and their imperfect sags would be lifted. Men would purchase this miracle device to get rid of love handles and gain those bulging biceps! And yet the Bible talks about such a tool for us. It isn't magical in the sense that gazing into it makes things happen. Nevertheless, it does come with power to change the one who understands how it works. It is this truth that began the process of changing my life.

As I have expressed already, my life began to spiral out of control. My hopes for the future were confronted by personal failures and disappointments. My life seemed to be overshadowed with a dark cloud of depression. I was taking medicine, going to counseling, and striving to "figure out" my life. I had even come to the place of contemplating suicide. God showed up with the mirror, and my life started a process of transformation that I want to share with you. The mirror is introduced in the Bible by James. James is believed to be the half-brother of Jesus by some. Read the following passage closely:

> *22 But be doers of the word, and not hearers only, deceiving yourselves. 23 For if anyone is a hearer of the word and not a doer, he is like a man who looks intently at his natural face in a mirror. 24 For he looks at himself and goes away and at once forgets what he was like. 25 But the one who looks into the perfect law, the law of liberty, and perseveres, being no hearer who forgets but a doer who acts, he will be blessed in his doing.* (James 1:22–25)

James says that when we read the Bible, it is as if we are peering into a mirror. He then takes it a step further and says what you see in the mirror of the Word is your "natural face." In other words, you see who you are by nature. When you read the Bible, you see your divine DNA. You see who you really are! Anything that doesn't measure up to the Word is the unnatural you. When I got this revelation, it changed the way I approached my devotions. I don't know about you, but I once read the Bible and left condemned because I never measured up. I would read and leave realizing how much different my life seemed to be. Of course, this approach wasn't uplifting and encouraging. It was more condemning than anything.

This is a religious view of the Bible. I encourage you to start reading the Bible with a different approach. God is trying to pull you forward, not push you away. He is not exposing your flaws in order to shame you. He is actually revealing to you your true identity! Anything other than what the Scriptures articulate is not the real you. For example, you may feel like you "can't win for losing."[24] You may be ashamed of all the times you have failed, and I'm sure you could tell me about missed opportunities and failures. As you read the Bible, you come across the passage that says, "You are more than a conqueror..." and feel condemned. You read about the "pure in heart" and feel so dirty. The Word is meant to reveal the "natural you" in order to propel you upward in glory. He is showing you the "truth," not to disqualify you but to release you to His potential.

You might say, as I did, "I read the Bible all the time, but nothing changes." I knew the Word. I read the Word. I memorized the Word. This is what distinguishes God's mirror from other mirrors—the mirror mindset will empower you to become you. Nevertheless, you are not transformed into His image simply by "looking" at the Bible. There is a key that unlocks its power.

Look again at the passage. James admonishes his readers to obey the Word, *not* just listen to it. He says that if you only hear the Word and do not do it, then you deceive yourself. It doesn't say that the devil deceives you. It doesn't blame your life on others' mistakes. It says that you deceive yourself. He continues by explaining that when a person doesn't reflect the Word of God in their lives, he or she is like a person who observes their natural face in a mirror and then goes away and immediately forgets what they are like. Notice it doesn't say that they forget who they are supposed to be like. No, they forget who they *really* are. The Word of God is a mirror that reflects the true identity of mankind. The Word reveals who you really are. The truth that you are reading should be the authority that you are obeying. When you obey the Word, you invoke its power to change you.

> *For the word of God is living and powerful, and sharper than any two-edged sword, piercing to the division of soul and spirit, and of joints and marrow, and is a discerner of the thoughts and intents of the heart.* (Hebrews 4:12 NKJV)

Don't miss this. As you read the Word, you are "seeing" the present components of your divine DNA. As you are "doing" the Word, your divine DNA is activated by dividing the soul from the spirit and rightly aligning with God and His Kingdom. When you look into the mirror of God's Word, you see your blessings, your intended fruitfulness, your promised dominion, keys to healthy relationships, and clarity for your divine purpose. There is nothing else that has to happen to make it a reality. It is already established in heaven! Unfortunately, heaven never makes it to the earth. Too many of us are satisfied with reducing our Christian experience to escaping the earth, but God wants you to experience His glory here! Sadly, we live in a world that Dr. Steven Land would call the "already, not yet."[25] The great tragedy is that too many people leave the earth without receiving God's promises.

James reveals the key that unlocks our divine DNA. As I share this, stay with me because your familiarity with the term could cause you to miss it. James says, "Don't be a hearer only, but be a doer of the Word." You are probably thinking, *I already knew I have to obey the Word.* I thought I understood this too. Then I began to put this principle to work in my life. Before this time my "obeying" was just a religious exercise and not a "Divine Transfer." I am going to be a little more transparent with you in the hope of showing you the "key" to my freedom.

Part of my struggle was what some may identify as OCD. Obsessive Compulsive Disorder impacted all of my life. To be quite honest with you, it played very easily into my fear-based life. I would "have to" wash my hands over and over again, take multiple showers, turn around and trace my steps over and over, etc. It was a tormenting life. I constantly second-guessed myself. For me, it wasn't just physical "dirt" I was anxious about. It was spiritual "dirt" as well. I continually felt condemned and guilty. In other words, I felt "dirty" on the inside. I couldn't get free. It had such a hold on me that it influenced my very identity.

I couldn't get free until I began to understand the mirror mindset. The mirror mindset is based on a principle that states that your reality is not based on what you see in you but what you see in Him. The realities of your earthly realm are always subservient to the truth of the heavenly realm. Obedience is the key that unlocks the door that grants heaven access to the earthly realm. You can read about it. You can meditate on it. You can think about it. Nevertheless, until you actually obey the truth of God's Word, there is a wall that separates Earth from heaven. Obeying God's Word invokes the authority of God's realm to establish itself on the earth. Conversely, obeying "Earth's words" empowers worldly laws to establish control.

The mirror mindset states that what you read about in the Word is the reality that God has already decreed for your life. Reading the Word is looking in the mirror and seeing your true image, while obeying the Word is the process that restores your current identity into your true identity. Obedience authorizes heaven's decree to manifest in the earthly realm. Let me break it down in a practical way.

I told you that I would *feel* like my hands were dirty, and so I would have to wash them over and over again. The truth was that my hands were clean. Nonetheless, my perception drove my reality, which was that they were dirty and needed to be washed. Have you ever faced something that you couldn't conquer? Have you ever dealt with an addition, a pattern, or a mindset that had such sway over your life? There is freedom for *any* bondage using the mirror mindset.

What gave me power over this "feeling"? I desperately obeyed the truth, and I say desperately because it was a fight. It wasn't easy. I didn't feel different at first. As a matter of fact, I still felt like my hands were dirty. But I had to resist my feeling so that fact could be established in my world. In a similar way, this is what happens spiritually. I may not feel strong or pure or hopeful, but I must choose to obey the Word in order to release the power of that word into my life. I have to resist living according to my feelings or my earthly sight.

> *Faith is the substance of things hoped for, the evidence of things not seen.* (Hebrews 11:1 NKJV)

The first key to unlocking your divine DNA is to live by faith and not fact. Dr. Pete Sulack would affirm that it is not necessary to deny the facts. Rather, it is necessary to live in such a way that you embrace a law that supersedes fact.[26] He illustrated this by stating that the "law of lift" supersedes the "law of gravity" when aerodynamics are at play. There may be situations that you are facing right now that seem impossible to overcome. People may have even told you to give up, that nothing will ever change. Know this—your divine DNA, when released, has authority over patterns, behaviors, earthly factors, chemical substances, and even generational curses. Jesus changed the rules! The power of blessing, increase, dominion, relationships, and divine purpose is waiting to go to work in your life.

Truth Is a Negative Word

Before we move on to other keys that will unlock your divine DNA, I want to show you another aspect of truth that affirms this idea that God's Word is a mirror reflecting who you really are. It has to do with the word "truth" itself. Jesus said, "…you will know the truth and the truth will set you free" (John 8:32). Truth is a powerful force that literally has the ability to transform your life. As you may know, "truth" is our English translation of the Greek word "aletheia." This is important because in the Greek, the prefix "a-" negates a word in the same way "non-" or "un-" negates English words. For example, unreachable is the reverse of reachable. In the same way, the term unstoppable is the opposite of stoppable.

Again, truth is a negative term. Let me explain it like this. The word aletheia is the combination of the negative "a" and "letheia." Therefore, to fully understand truth, we must understand what it is not. The root word, lethe, will help give us clarity. In Ancient Greek, lethe means forgetfulness or concealment. This term is so significant that in Greek mythology, there is a river called Lethe located in the Hades underworld. Interestingly, when someone drank from this river, it was believed to cause forgetfulness.[27] This is going to blow your mind! The negative of lethe is "unforgetfulness" or "unconcealed." Or I could say that "truth" is "not-forgetting."

James said that a person who reads the Word but doesn't obey it is like a man who looks at his "natural face" and then goes away and FORGETS what he was like. When you know the truth, you quit forgetting who you really are! When you know the truth, the eyes of your heart start "seeing" your true identity. Knowing the truth empowers you to unlock your divine DNA and live life to the full. You become free to be. You become free to live in such a way that brings glory and honor to your Creator. Outside of this truth, we live below our intended glory. When we see the truth as expressed in God's Word, it empowers us to be transformed from glory to glory. One translation actually reads, "ever increasing glory" (See 2 Corinthians 3:18).

The truth makes it possible to unlock blessings that are in heavenly places and releases them into the earth.

Truth makes you free to increase in favor with both God and man. Truth positions you to rule in life as God intended. Truth brings healing to relationships that are wounded because of the false cover of shame and blame. Lastly, truth enables you to fulfill every ounce of divine purpose. Truth sets you free to be who you were originally intended to be. It is time for you to quit drinking from the river of forgetfulness and to allow God to open your eyes to who you really are!

CHAPTER 13
THE TAKE METHOD
A STRATEGY FOR BUILDING HEALTHY RELATIONSHIPS

"Love never fails."

—1 Corinthians 13:8

The idea behind The Take Method is twofold. There are two primary definitions for the word take. First, you are receiving something or laying hold of something. In this concept, we recognize that cultivating relationships can never happen from a passive stance. In relationships, we have to work at it. Sometimes we have to be aggressive in our efforts to restore and repair broken relationships. Intentionality in relationships cannot be underestimated. I encourage you to get ready to take hold of healthy relationships.

The second connotation of the word take is "to carry" or "bring." Someone might say, "I am taking this to work." In other words, the take method empowers us to move forward in our relationships rather than staying in a cycle of apathy, abuse, or mistrust. With the principles that follow, you will be empowered to "take" your relationships from where they are now to where God intended for them to be. You were created to have healthy relationships, but our society and our churches have become so accustomed to dysfunctional relationships that we call it normal.

God never intended for hatred, drama, distrust, fear, and hurt to be the "normal" aspect of a relationship. Sometimes in response to failed relationships, hurts, and wounds by others, we attempt to dismiss by sighing, "It is what it is." The Father created you with the capacity to have a relationship just like He has with Jesus and the Holy Spirit. In God's relationship, there is no jealousy, backbiting, separation, or abuse. They are perfect in unity. Jesus understands the power of this oneness and that it is so significant to our expression of glory that He prayed, "Father, make them one even as you and I are one." Jesus is praying for you to have healthy relationships. It is up to you to "Amen" that prayer and *take* your relationships to the place and purpose for which He created you. You can't make unity happen, but the Bible charges us live at peace with others as much as it up to us (See Romans 12:18).

Disclaimer: The following principles are not necessarily intended to be followed in order. Nor is it suggested that all 10 principles would have to be employed in order to overcome a conflict. These 10 principles, called "The Take Method," are a set of keys meant to give you the power to unlock the divine DNA of God's intention in your relationships.

Principle #1: Take It to God

Proverbs 3:6 says, "In all your ways acknowledge Him and He will direct your path." You and I need God's help as we pursue healthy relationships. This is important whether we are trying to bring healing to a relationship or desiring to start a relationship correctly. Rick Warren offers several steps for repairing broken relationships.[28] His steps informed the framework for these principles. He says, "The first biblical step toward restoring a relationship is to talk to God before talking to the person."[29] Acknowledging God first gives you an advantage. It is your personal invite for God to release grace and resources to work in the situation.

First things are always significant things. First impressions. First love. First kisses. Therefore, it is important in the work of cultivating healthy relationships that you have God's perspective. Oftentimes, if you go to others first, then you will gain opinions and mindsets that are contrary to truth. Only God can see the heart. Only God knows what is really happening under the surface of our interactions with each other. Far too often our first deduction of a matter is stained with fallen perspectives, and taking it to God first gives the relationship the best opportunity to move forward.

Principle #2: Take Responsibility

After you have looked up to God, it is time to look inside to your own heart. What part of brokenness are you guilty of? "You must confess your faults instead of blame shifting."[30] Remember, the blame game began in the Garden with the first broken relationship. As Paul charges, we should "examine ourselves." This is exactly in line with the way Jesus taught us to approach the Father in prayer. He said, "Pray like this…forgive us our trespasses as we forgive those who have trespassed against us" (See Matthew 6:12). Taking responsibility for our own actions first will cultivate the right environment for healing.

Principle #3: Take the First Step

Aaron Reisinger said, "Many times we must take the initiative in forgiveness even when we are the ones who have been done wrong."[31] This approach aligns with the same attitude that Christ had when He came to the earth. As the only perfect one, He had every right to ignore the predicament of mankind and choose not to come to our aid. On the contrary, He let go of His rights and took the initiative to restore a relationship with us. Listen to this verse that describes the commitment Christ had in reaching us even when we didn't deserve a chance.

> *For while we were still weak, at the right time Christ died for the ungodly. For one will scarcely die for a righteous person—though perhaps for a good person one would dare even to die—but God shows his love for us in that while we were still sinners, Christ died for us.* (Romans 5:6–8)

We should follow His example and do the same for the people in our lives—even when they don't deserve it. What can you do to take the first step to heal that relationship?

Principle #4: Take Care

This principle requires that you and I lean on God's grace. We must be very careful when we are in a conflict with another person. A broken relationship is first and foremost a symptom of a broken person. We must be careful how we handle the situation, realizing that we are handling a soul that is dear to the Father. We must look past the moment and past the offense in order to see the child of God formed in His image (See Genesis 9:6). The Apostle Paul commands us to "bear one another's burdens, and so fulfill the law of Christ" (Galatians 6:2). If we make it our priority to take care of the person, the conflict will be much more likely to take care of itself.

Principle #5: Take a Break

You may have heard it said, "Time heals all things." I don't believe this is universally or exhaustively true. Nevertheless, we would be much closer to healthy relationships if we would take a break and allow our emotions to calm before we continue in some conversations.

On the other hand, it is important for us to not wait too long in our process of reconciliation. Avoiding dealing with offenses oftentimes will set you up for a devastating outcome. The Apostle Paul warns not to allow the "sun [to] go down on your anger" (See Ephesians 4:26). Along the same counsel, the writer of Hebrews warns against allowing our offenses to take root in our hearts. We should rather work to be at peace with everyone. Bitterness in our hearts will inevitably spew over and damage ourselves and the important people in our lives (See Hebrews 12:14-15).

Principle #6: Take Cover

The idea behind this principle is to put everything under the authority and protection of love. Let your words, your actions, and your heart be submissive to love. In 1 Peter 4:8, Peter declares that "love covers a multitude of sins." The opening quote to this chapter reminds us that "love never fails." When we put into practice the mirror mindset and act according to truth and not what we see, it is much easier to employ love as our strategy to solve our differences. As mentioned earlier, love is a powerful force that either constrains us or compels us according to the need of the moment. Love is the key to healing and avoiding dysfunctional relationships. Broken relationships are the symptoms of broken people, but love will heal that brokenness.

Let me give one last thought regarding love. As much as "love never fails," it also "never ends." What do I mean? When I think about "love never failing" I am encouraged by the fact that love always wins. When you choose to love, you choose a guaranteed victory. It conquers fear and hurt and disappointment. Secondly, love never ends. This means love never runs out. The bank of love is never overdrawn. There is always enough love to satisfy any and every relationship need. When a person says, "I just don't love them anymore." It is not because there is no love to draw from. Love is a resource that is always available.

You were created for healthy relationships. Your responsibility is to put every sin, every hurt, and every failure under the cover of love, and you will find that your relationships will be stronger and able to endure the trials and storms of life.

Principle #7: Take the Trash Out

In 1 Corinthians 13:5, we learn that one of the attributes of love is that it "keeps no record of wrongs." This is important when it comes to moving forward in our relationships with one another. Every time we are wounded by someone, we need to take the trash out. In other words, we shouldn't maintain a list to pull out every time we have an argument. Past mistakes and offenses should never have the opportunity to be brought up again as a weapon to win the next argument. We need to get rid of "trash" that is left hanging around, or it will spoil our next meal.

Right now, before you go any further, make a list of any hurts, wounds, offenses, or things that tend to come up each time you have an argument. Now take the list and declare over each item, "You are forgiven." Then rip the paper up and throw it in the trash!

TAKE THE TRASH OUT EXERCISE

"Love Keeps No Record of Wrongs"
—1 Corinthians 13:5

1. _____
2. _____
3. _____
4. _____
5. _____
6. _____
7. _____
8. _____
9. _____
10. _____

Now speak each item out loud and then say, "You are forgiven!"

Now, it's time to take the trash out! Take the piece of paper, rip it up, and throw it in the trash.

Tip: Make a copy of this page for future use. The reality is that hurts are a part of relationships. We have to continually choose to forgive and move on.

Principle #8: Take Time

In covenant relationships like marriage, God can use our hurts along with some time to produce a stronger bond. Making the commitment to work through our problems actually cultivates a healthier, deeper relationship. Unfortunately, connections with this kind of loyalty are few and far between. The reality is that relationships take time. Relationships are not built or rebuilt overnight. We must see building relationships like building a house. The stronger the foundation, the greater the structure. Building deep relationships is worth the investment but requires a significant deposit of time. First Thessalonians 5:14 reads, "...be patient with them all." The "all" that the writer is referring to are identified as the idle, the fainthearted, and the weak. False expectations drive us into disappointment, but if we can look at others with our own weaknesses in mind, it will provide the proper context to establish healthy expectations of others. When we approach our relationships with the posture to give rather than take, it enables us to serve others and to add value to them. We become agents of healing rather than contributors to dysfunction.

Principle #9: Take a Map

Wouldn't it be nice if every new relationship came with an instruction guide? Or even better, what if our relationships came with a GPS system that said, "Take the next exit." Unfortunately, a guide like this isn't provided each time we start a relationship. Nevertheless, we must learn to honor the principles found in God's Word. We can use the instructions in the Bible to provide a road map to guide our path. These principles establish boundaries that work like the yellow lines on a highway. They will keep us in our lane and help us avoid dangers.

Our associations with people must always have boundaries. For example, the Apostle Paul, giving instruction to individuals who are considering marriage, says the following: "Do not be unequally yoked with unbelievers. For what partnership has righteousness with lawlessness? Or what fellowship has light with darkness? What accord has Christ with Belial? Or what portion does a believer share with an unbeliever?" (2 Corinthians 6:14-16). Yes, this refers to marital covenants. However, I would suggest that this could be applied to business partnerships or any other legal connection that demands trust and loyalty. This principle should be applied to any relationship of trust.

Another type of boundary that must be honored are boundaries that protect one's commitment to another person. As it relates to marriage, husbands and wives should establish rules that protect their relationship. On a practical level, this would be actions like not emailing, texting, or Facebooking an individual of the opposite sex without our spouse's knowledge. We should always provide our mate with access to these links. Usernames, passwords, etc., should be available to the other person. Keeping the light on gives no place for darkness to show up. Boundaries are always set to protect, to provide space to dwell, and to identify ownership. Allow these three principles to guide you in establishing relationships with others. For those under your care, like children or students, it is your responsibility to establish healthy relationships for them.

Principle #10: Take a Hike

This last principle is one that must be used at times in order to protect other relationships. Due to the brokenness of some of the people in our lives, a boundary is not enough to protect us. Sometimes it is necessary to completely remove a person from our lives. The Apostle Paul speaks to this in 2 Corinthians 6:17–18: "Therefore go out from their midst, and be separate from them, says the Lord, and touch no unclean thing; then I will welcome you, and I will be a father to you, and you shall be sons and daughters to me, says the Lord Almighty."

There are certain people who are so toxic that allowing them to stay in connection to you will lead to further harm and abuse. If you are in a relationship that you feel could necessitate this kind of action, I would encourage you to find someone you can trust and ask them to help. In cases of physical abuse, it may be necessary to involve the authorities. Remember, you have a purpose to express to this world, and you cannot allow another person to keep you from shining for the glory of God. The world is waiting on you!

These ten principles, though not exhaustive, will hopefully guide you along a path to establishing healthy relationships with the people in your life. Remember, God created you for relationships. Healthy relationships are part of your divine DNA and are necessary for you to fulfill your divine purpose. God's grace will help you connect with the right people. If you need a "tribe" of people to support you on the journey, why not consider becoming a part of a group of people striving to unlock their divine DNA? You can find out more information at www.tonycolson.com.

CHAPTER 14
PRINCIPLES, PRIORITIES, AND PURSUITS
A PRACTICAL GUIDE TO ACHIEVING YOUR POTENTIAL

In this final chapter, my goal is to place keys into your hands that will assist in unlocking your divine DNA. I wish it was as simple as an enchanted formula or saying a magical phrase, but it's not. Nevertheless, it is still possible. With this practical guide, you will be able to achieve your potential in Christ. Your life can begin to reflect the beautiful masterpiece that your Creator intended. In the next few pages, I am going to share with you principles that I believe are keys to unlocking your future. These are keys that God has decreed to work in our lives. And when put into practice, there is a guarantee that heavenly resources will be released into your earthly experience.

I will begin with sharing principles that I believe are universal and relate to everyone. Next I will share the pursuits that I have chosen to focus on in order to fulfill my purpose. Then I will share the priorities or daily disciplines that I have identified as the small steps to take toward the glorious transformation. Lastly, I will guide you to be able to identify your own pursuits and priorities as you, too, begin to put the keys to work in your life. It won't be long before you start seeing God's glory increase, and you will soon be walking in your divine DNA—blessing, fruitfulness, dominion, healthy relationships, and purpose.

Let me start by listing the keys that will unlock your divine DNA:

- Kingdom Priority
- Discipline Demand
- Stewardship Mandate
- Suffering Reality
- Servant Leadership
- Unlimited Possibility
- Seed Replaces Need
- Love Never Fails

Kingdom Priority

The power of heaven is locked in the government of the Kingdom. This means that you have to unlock it by using keys. Jesus taught us to seek first the Kingdom of God and His righteousness and then all these things would be added to us (See Matthew 6:33). It is important for you to make this adjustment in your life. If you want the blessing of the King, you have to seek His

Kingdom first. This establishes the first priorities of all priorities. Everything you do, say, and pursue must be under the covering of the Kingdom.

In all your ways acknowledge him, and he will make straight your paths. (Proverbs 3:6)

Every morning I bow before God and acknowledge that I need Him. I simply confess that I need Him to be His son and to be a good husband, father, pastor, author, and professor. I cannot fulfill these roles adequately without Him directing my path. He is first and foremost. His plan supersedes my plan. His will overrules my desires. He and His kingdom take priority over everything else in my life. Another key to understand is that God is successful everywhere. God always gains victory over his enemies whether they are in heaven trying to take over the throne or in hell trying to hold on to some keys. And He will never lead you into defeat.[32] This posture in life is necessary if the resources to live life to the full are to be released. As Myles Munroe said, "The maintenance of the rightly aligned relationship with a governing authority" must be maintained in order to be granted "governmental privileges."[33] Most of my life has been spent seeking my interests, needs, and wants before the Kingdom. This approach, in essence, forfeits the grace of God from working fully in my life. Again, I am not talking about the grace that gets you into heaven. I am talking about the grace that gets heaven into you.

When you put the Kingdom first in your life, you guarantee that the Kingdom will last in your life. What you invest the most in is what you reap the most from. The first key to start unlocking your future is to examine your priorities. How do you invest your time? Where do you spend your money? What would you spend money on if you could only buy one thing? These questions will help you determine your first priority.

Discipline Demand

Discipline is an important key that unlocks your future. You have to decide to live today for tomorrow so that tomorrow will become today. Too often we live our lives merely focused on today's pleasures or today's problems. The discipline demand key gives you access to the reality that you cannot get by living for the moment. Being disciplined is one's willingness to submit themselves to an authority that cannot be seen in order to overpower the rule of what can be seen. Paul speaks to this reality in the following passage:

> *Do you not know that in a race all the runners run, but only one receives the prize? So run that you may obtain it. Every athlete exercises self-control in all things. They do it to receive a perishable wreath, but we an imperishable. So I do not run aimlessly; I do not box as one beating the air. But I discipline my body and keep it under control, lest after preaching to others I myself should be disqualified.* (1 Corinthians 9:24–27)

Paul connects our earthly disciplines to our eternal position. This may be hard for some of us to understand. The reality is that how we live on Earth determines our ultimate standing in heaven. And according to this scripture, the way we discipline our bodies will impact our ability to fulfill our purpose.

Stewardship Mandate

Stewardship is an interesting concept. Stewardship is managing something for someone else and being responsible for what is not yours. The stewardship mandate helps us understand that the way we manage our responsibilities impacts whether or not we will be positioned to achieve our full potential. Jesus said it like this: "And if you have not been faithful in that which is another's, who will give you that which is your own?" (Luke 16:12).

As you are preparing for your future and your calling, it is essential that you serve those in your life the way you want to be served one day. Take a moment to examine your relationships. How do you submit to those over you? How do you treat the property of your workplace? How do you care for your community? Your stewardship of what is someone else's has a direct implication on what is released into your life.

Suffering Reality

Why is pain necessary? This is perhaps one of the hardest components of maturing in life. One of the keys that unlocks the door to greatness is your willingness to endure hardships and pain. It would be wonderful if we were able to avoid difficulties, conflicts, and trials. Nevertheless, the best things in life often come with a price. The transition from one glory to another involves a journey down difficult paths. Everyone faces this "suffering reality"; however, this suffering opens the door for greater things: "For I consider that the sufferings of this present time are not worth comparing with the glory that is to be revealed to us" (Romans 8:18).

Maybe you have seen those commercials for the "miracle pill." Wouldn't it be nice if there was a "glory pill"? I could say, "Take two of these, and glory comes in the morning." Unfortunately, there is no such invention. In order to get in shape, you will have to endure the pain of working out. In order to finish your book, you will have to say no to your friends and not go to the movie. Pain is part of the process. It is one of the keys to unlocking glory in your life. There is no magical pill. Instead, it is these trials and moments of difficulty that produce glory in your life.

Servant Leadership

Another key to unlocking God's greatness is servant leadership. The first scripture God spoke to me is found in 1 Corinthians 9:19. It says, "For though I am free from all, I have made myself a servant to all, that I might win more of them." Kingdom servanthood is a choice that we make. When we learn to posture ourselves in a position of service to others, we employ a key that has great paybacks. This principle is important when trying to establish relationships with people. Intentional servanthood is the express representation of heaven on the earth. Jesus modeled this priority when He said, "… But whoever would be great among you must be your servant, and whoever would be first among you must be your slave, even as the Son of Man came not to be served but to serve, and to give his life as a ransom for many" (Matthew 20:26b–28).

Oftentimes we must step back and realize that our relationships and actions on Earth need to be driven by a heavenly perspective. This key will unlock the door for us to have relationships that match heaven. Also, it will help us to win others to the Kingdom!

Unlimited Possibility

Anything is possible! This may be one of the most exciting keys that God has offered us. The key of faith helps us to realize that nothing is impossible with God (See Luke 1:37). Why is this an important key? Expectations create the atmosphere for your reality, so it is essential that you change your expectations for your life. Your divine DNA comes powerfully charged with possibility, and when you release your divine DNA through the key of faith (unlimited possibility), absolutely nothing is beyond your grasp. This key is not dependent upon a track record of performance. It is not controlled by the past. It is the key that invites the future into your present.

> **Expectations create the atmosphere for your reality.**

And Jesus said to him, 'If you can'! All things are possible for one who believes. (Mark 9:23)

In other words, you plus belief equals possibility. In you is everything you need to make impossible things possible. God has placed inside of you the seed of faith so you can use the key of faith to bring about the reward of faith. The reward of faith is literally "all things."

Seed Replaces Need

This is a profound key that we must employ in our journey to glory. The "seed replaces need" principle simply states that you must let go of something to receive something better. The following is a lengthy passage, but I believe it is necessary to draw your attention to the biblical principle.

> *6 The point is this: whoever sows sparingly will also reap sparingly, and whoever sows bountifully will also reap bountifully. 7 Each one must give as he has decided in his heart, not reluctantly or under compulsion, for God loves a cheerful giver. 8 And God is able to make all grace abound to you, so that having all sufficiency in all things at all times, you may abound in every good work. 9 As it is written, 'He has distributed freely, he has given to the poor; his righteousness endures forever.' 10 He who supplies seed to the sower and bread for food will supply and multiply your seed for sowing and increase the harvest of your righteousness. 11 You will be enriched in every way to be generous in every way, which through us will produce thanksgiving to God. 12 For the ministry of this service is not only supplying the needs of the saints but is also overflowing in many thanksgivings to God. 13 By their approval of this service, they will glorify God because of your submission that comes from your confession of the gospel of Christ, and the generosity of your contribution for them and for all others, 14 while they long for you and pray for you, because of the surpassing grace of God upon you.* (2 Corinthians 9:6-14)

Seed is your currency to acquiring overflow. Seed is necessary to transition you from a life of need to a life of more than enough. Seed replaces need. I want to encourage you to examine your resources and designate some of it as seed. Too many of us consume our seed, which in effect forfeits our harvest. There are great teachings about "sowing and reaping." Let me just encourage you with these reminders:

- You reap in direct proportion to how you sow.
- Your attitude when you give matters.
- The harvest is a multiplied return of what you have sown.
- Your seeds are from God, and your harvest is from God.
- Your increase is for God's glory.

Love Never Fails

"Love never fails" may be the most quoted phrase in weddings. The statement is so familiar that we can miss the power of it. Think about it just for a moment. "Love never fails." Never is a strong word. Being a biblical truth, it was not written as poetic virtuoso. It's intention goes beyond imagery to reality. It is truth. "Love never fails."

Unfortunately, in our culture, our understanding is influenced by expressions wrongly called love and yet is far from it. Love is oftentimes reduced to an emotion that is expressed as "butterflies" in a person's stomach. Love is related both to the relationships of husbands and wives as well as our stomachs' craving for a fast food burger. We love donuts and children and roller coasters and lost people. The same word somehow blends together to communicate connections toward such different realities.

Loving donuts is not what we are referring to. Love is best articulated in 1 Corinthians 13 with statements like "Love is not rude, it is not self seeking, doesn't keep a record of wrongs, it hopes all things, endures all things, and bears all things." This kind of love cannot be conquered. It cannot be overdrawn. It never runs out. It always prevails.

This key—love never fails—enables you to always live life as a victor. Living from love is the key to allowing love to lead you on a path of constant victory.

Adjusting your life to honor these principles will guarantee the unlocking of your divine DNA. These keys will unlock blessing, fruitfulness, dominion, healthy relationships, and fulfilled purpose. You already have everything you need—these keys simply release what is in you to operate fully.

Disclaimer: It will not happen overnight. The way life works is by progressive transformation. You initial efforts of change may see little or no results in the natural. Do not give up! Do not quit. Your harvest is transferring—the divine transfer will come! Do you see it? Look back at the mirror, and see who you really are. Take control of your life, and use these principles (keys) to unlock your divine DNA.

In the final section, I want to lead you through a practical exercise in order to embrace the pursuits that match your purpose. Lastly, I want you to identify the priorities that must be honored for you to go from "glory to glory."

Why Are You Here?

First of all, reflecting on the principles above, what are *your* pursuits? Your pursuits are the roles and goals you need to focus on. Embracing this kind of focus will help you steward the call of God on your life. I am going to share a couple of mine in order to help you identify yours.

UNLOCKING YOUR DIVINE DNA LAUNCH TEAM

Join Tony's Launch Team Today!

Here's what you get:

- **Free** 2 Months Access to the Transformation Tribe. This is a private Facebook group where Pastor Tony will teach the principles of Unlocking Your Divine DNA answering your questions personally.
- **Free** Study Guide / Workbook that you can go through with a small group or by yourself. (Available in Fall 2017)

Here's all we request from you:

- Sign up at **tonycolson.com**
- Share at least one of Tony's Social Media post each week or share a quote from the book each week using the hashtag #UnlockingYourDivineDNA until August 14.
- We ask you to write a Review at Amazon.com / Barnes and Noble on August 14 – official release date of Tony's new book.

Don't wait. Join now!

tonycolson.com

For example, one of my pursuits is to be a healthy husband. For me, being a healthy husband looks like the following. As a husband, my aim is to be loving, caring, protective, a provider, strong, confident, and fun.

Am I perfect as a husband? Far from it! However, this is my pursuit. This is what I am pressing toward. When I evaluate my life as a husband, this provides the questions I can ask myself. Have I been loving toward my wife? Am I protecting my wife? Will this job provide for my home? The pursuits based on the principles inform my decisions. The principles are the guard rails, and the pursuits are the lanes in which I live. When I embrace and promote these roles in my life, my earthly experiences are ordered by this reality rather than other distractions.

Another pursuit of mine is having financial success. This pursuit creates an expectation for my life that contradicts the poverty mindset that I have lived under for many years. As a pastor, I had embraced a mindset that I should not be rich or comfortable in life. This perspective was not based on God's desire for me but on a false humility that is contrary to what God truly wants. I cannot fulfill my purpose without resources. I cannot acquire resources without financial success!

How about you? What are the pursuits that should be "lanes" you stay in on this journey called life? Take a few moments and mediate on these "keys" above, and determine which roles and goals you need to pursue:

PURSUITS

My Roles and Goals That Will Express God's Image in the Earth

ROLE / GOAL	WHAT THIS WOULD LOOK LIKE
1. _____	_____
2. _____	_____
3. _____	_____
4. _____	_____
5. _____	_____

The last section of this chapter is where discipline promotes your success. Your commitment to daily priorities will determine whether or not you enter your future or continue to "window shop" through life. Again, examining the principles and pursuits above will help you identify essential priorities that must be followed.

Priorities will do a few things. First of all, priorities create boundaries. Next, priorities establish value. Lastly, priorities give you clarity on what is important to your life. Establishing priorities empowers you to say no to intruders trying to rob you of your destiny. Let me encourage you not to make too many priorities. It would be better for you to start with three or four that you know you can accomplish rather than

> Establishing priorities empowers you to say no to intruders trying to rob you of your destiny.

listing 20–25 priorities that will overwhelm you and cause you to give up.

As an example, here are a couple of mine that support my pursuits and are in line with the principles listed above:

1. <u>Get Adequate Sleep</u> –7 hours/night, go to bed early, rise early) (Principle – Stewardship Mandate; Pursuit – Healthy Husband, Physically Fit)
2. <u>Touch Lives</u> –send cards, text wife encouraging words, tell someone Happy Birthday on Facebook (Principle – Servant Leadership, Love Never Fails; Pursuit – Healthy Husband, Kingdom Leader)

I would suggest that you list no more than 8–10 priorities. Your priorities should be revisited on a regular basis in order to be established in your life. These are the practical actions that you are going to take in order to move your life closer day by day to the intention God has for you! Here is a worksheet to help you:

PRIORITIES

My daily actions that will move me toward the intention God has for me:

1. _____
   Principle: _____
   Pursuit: _____
2. _____
   Principle: _____
   Pursuit: _____

3. _____
    Principle: _____
    Pursuit: _____
4. _____
    Principle: _____
    Pursuit: _____
5. _____
    Principle: _____
    Pursuit: _____
6. _____
    Principle: _____
    Pursuit: _____

God has great things in store for you—greatness! You are beginning a journey of unlocking your divine DNA. You can't even imagine what God has prepared for you. It is right around the corner. Don't wait! Look into the mirror—the door is wide open. Your divine DNA is now unlocked. Welcome to your future!

For more help on going further on this journey, connect with me at tonycolson.com.

EPILOGUE

A VISION OF GLORY

EPILOGUE
A VISION OF GLORY
WHAT IF EVERYONE UNLOCKED THEIR DIVINE DNA?

Unlocking *your* divine DNA has a purpose that goes beyond you. The more people who start unlocking their divine DNA, the more something powerful begins to happen. There is a collective power to people made whole who are also made one. Something miraculous happens when a group of people start operating under the full potential of God's divine image. Life is never about just one person. It is always about the magical dance of unity motivated by love. I am going to call this the "love dance." There are not many things more elegant or more beautiful than the symmetry involved between dancers who are perfectly in step.

A popular television show called *Dancing with the Stars* popularized the dance between two individuals. Nevertheless, what is even more impressive is the dance of multiple individuals who seemed to be connected by invisible strings…or perhaps the water dance routines of synchronized swimmers. The body of Christ is created to operate in this way—beautiful, powerful, supernatural oneness.

One of my professors, Dr. Wesley Pinkham, owned a yacht that was named after a Greek term that captured this kind of divine intent. His yacht was called Perichoresis. It is one word that illustrates this kind of God-sized unity. Perichoresis can be seen in the relationship between the Father, the Son, and the Holy Spirit. Perfect unity. No competition, only completion. Only complementing of one another. When we finally learn to unlock God's divine DNA—not just individually but collectively—this is what happens.

Something glorious happens when a lot of people "get it." This is what Jesus was referring to when He said, "The gates of hell will not prevail against [the church]" (See Matthew 16:18). When we get this and begin the love dance, there is nothing that hell possesses that can compete. Love never fails. Love casts out all fear. Love heals. Love gives when there is lack. Love constrains, and love compels. And when love is being administered through a unified multitude, a powerful, supernatural force is released that nothing can stop. This is the vision of glory. Two passages of Scripture articulate this vision biblically:

> *10 All mine are yours, and yours are mine, and I am glorified in them. 11 And I am no longer in the world, but they are in the world, and I am coming to you. Holy Father, keep them in your name, which you have given me, that they may be one, even as we are one. 12 While I was with them, I kept them in your name, which you*

have given me. I have guarded them, and not one of them has been lost except the son of destruction, that the Scripture might be fulfilled. 13 But now I am coming to you, and these things I speak in the world, that they may have my joy fulfilled in themselves. 14 I have given them your word, and the world has hated them because they are not of the world, just as I am not of the world. 15 I do not ask that you take them out of the world, but that you keep them from the evil one. 16 They are not of the world, just as I am not of the world. 17 Sanctify them in the truth; your word is truth. 18 As you sent me into the world, so I have sent them into the world. 19 And for their sake I consecrate myself, that they also may be sanctified in truth. 20 "I do not ask for these only, but also for those who will believe in me through their word, 21 that they may all be one, just as you, Father, are in me, and I in you, that they also may be in us, so that the world may believe that you have sent me. 22 The glory that you have given me I have given to them, that they may be one even as we are one, 23 I in them and you in me, that they may become perfectly one, so that the world may know that you sent me and loved them even as you loved me. 24 Father, I desire that they also, whom you have given me, may be with me where I am, to see my glory that you have given me because you loved me before the foundation of the world. 25 O righteous Father, even though the world does not know you, I know you, and these know that you have sent me. 26 I made known to them your name, and I will continue to make it known, that the love with which you have loved me may be in them, and I in them. (John 17:10-26)

In this passage of Scripture, we see that glory to God is granted through His people. Sure, God could force His hand and demand glory to His name (which no doubt one day will happen). But for now, God is looking for a people who will live in such a way that when others observe their ways, their words, and their lifestyles, they by default give glory to God—their God. In this passage, we hear the appeal of Jesus to His Father. He asks for their unity, their protection, their glory, and their love to be present in them. These elements are necessary for the world to be convinced of the truthfulness of God.

Next we see the work of a glorious church in Paul's letter to the Ephesians:

> *11 And he gave the apostles, the prophets, the evangelists, the shepherds and teachers, 12 to equip the saints for the work of ministry, for building up the body of Christ, 13 until we all attain to the unity of the faith and of the knowledge of the Son of God, to mature manhood, to the measure of the stature of the fullness of Christ, 14 so that we may no longer be children, tossed to and fro by the waves and carried about by every wind of doctrine, by human cunning, by craftiness in deceitful schemes. 15 Rather, speaking the truth in love, we are to grow up in every way into him who is the head, into Christ, 16 from whom the whole body, joined and held together by every joint with which it is equipped, when each part is working properly, makes the body grow so that it builds itself up in love.* (Ephesians 4:11-16)

In this passage, we see some of the same elements found in John 17. We see unity, love, maturity, and supernatural glory of people being built into a powerful force of ministry. Ministry is not just a word for things that happen on Sundays at church. Ministry is the activity of a people committed to serving broken people in order to help them meet a God who heals.

The vision of a glorious church can be seen in the words of both Paul and Jesus. This vision involves love, unity, maturation, and supernatural power operating in an earthly realm, and it enjoys divine protection from the works of the enemy. The enemy incites disunity, hatred, and acts of irresponsibility, which produce weak, powerless Christians and churches. Thus, when the world observes us, the body of Christ, they don't see glory. They see something shameful.

I encourage you today to commit to the process needed to unlock your divine DNA. I pray that you, through this journey, will empower others to rise up to be the Church, the glorious Church, that Christ is building in the earth to demonstrate His glory. God intends to use you to show off His wisdom and power!

Here—take the keys and unlock your future! Unlock your divine DNA, and become everything that you were created for! Then go set your family and friends free as well. The world is waiting on you!

ENDNOTES

1. http://stmatthews-bowie.org/the-glory-of-god-is-the-human-person-fully-alive-st-irenaeus/
2. http://health.howstuffworks.com/human-body/parts/16-unusual-facts-about-the-human-body.htm - page=16
3. http://www.azquotes.com/quote/977264
4. This quote is from my childhood pastor, Gerald McGinnis, that I heard during one of his messages.
5. Dr. Wes Pinkham charted these attributes in his work, *Identity-Formation: The Journey toward Person-Formation*. Chattanooga: JttH Ministries, 2001. Unpublished manuscript, 211. Dr. Pinkham had taken the attributes from Arthur Holmes' work, *The Idea of a Christian College* (See next footnote).
6. Arthur F. Holmes, *The Idea of A Christian College*. Grand Rapids: WM. B. Eerdmans Publishing CO., 1975, 33-45.
7. The term, "response-able," was introduced to me by Dr. Wes Pinkham during my doctoral studies at Kings University in Van Nuys, California.

8. Konnikova, Maria. "The Power of Touch." The New Yorker. Accessed February 12, 2016. http://www.newyorker.com/science/maria-konnikova/power-touch
9. http://www.cell.com/neuron/fulltext/S0896-6273(14)00387-0
10. http://preventdisease.com/news/14/012314_9-Reasons-Need-Giving-Receiving-Hugs-Everyday.shtml
11. http://www.christianpost.com/news/craig-groeschel-tells-church-leaders-to-embrace-pain-81357/
12. Chaplain Carey Robertson was a minister on staff at Brownsville Assembly of God in Pensacola, Florida. He shared this insight with me during a personal meeting.
13. https://www.google.com/search?q=definition+of+position&oq=definition+of+position&aqs=chrome..69i57j0l5.11239j0j4&sourceid=chrome&ie=UTF-8
14. DNA: definition acquired from google.com. Search related to define: dna
15. https://lionalert.org/page/predatory-behaviour
16. Mowry LaCugna. The Trinity. New York: Harper Collins, 1993, 274.
17. Kary Oberbrunner is my writing coach and founder of the Igniting Souls tribe. You can find out more information about him at http://www.karyoberbrunner.com/
18. See the New International Version and the American King James Version.
19. Tenney, Merrill. New Testament Survey. Grand Rapids; Wm. B. Eerdmans Publishing Co., 1985, 245-247.
20. "The Village of Arbour Trails." Vol. 1, Issue 2. Page 9.
21. This idea of past scripts was introduced by Dr. Wes Pinkham during my doctoral program at King's University in Van Nuys, California.
22. Jesus is the Door. Pastor Ron Carpenter teaches that we are not to stay at the door. Jesus is the one who gives us access to the Kingdom. We would never go

to our earthly father's house and then stay at the door. No, we will enter in and enjoy his house!
23. In part 2 of the Levels Series, Pastor Ron Carpenter declared that God sent Adam to govern the earth. April 2, 2017. Preached at Redemption Church (Greenville, SC).
24. This was one of my grandmother's favorite sayings.
25. I first learned this term during one of my Master of Divinity classes taught by Steven Land. He writes about it in his book, *Pentecostal Spirituality*. (Sheffield Press, 1993).
26. Pete Sulack, "God's Laws for Health Summit", Living Waters Retreat Center. February 3–4, 2017.
27. http://www.mythweb.com/encyc/gallery/lethe_c.html
28. http://www.faithgateway.com/restoring-broken-fellowship/ - .WKd6cRIrIjd
29. http://rickwarren.org/devotional/english/restoring-relationships-talk-to-god_639
30. http://www.covenantkeepers.org/online-articles/42-conflict-resolution/313-how-do-you-resolve-conflicts-in-a-biblical-way
31. http://www.holybiblesays.org/articles.php?ID=419
32. See 2 Corinthians 5:14 and Revelation 1:17,18.
33. Myles, Munroe. Kingdom Principles Study Guide. Destiny Image Publishers (Shippensburg, PA),18.
34. https://publications.nigms.nih.gov/insidethecell/chapter4.html
35. Pastor Gray was one of the speakers at the 2016 ARC Conference held at Church of the Highlands in April, 2016 (Birmingham, AL)
36. Pastor Robert Sheppard preached this during a sermon while he was the Campus Pastor for Lee University during the early 1990's. (Cleveland, TN).

ABOUT THE AUTHOR

Dr. Tony Colson is currently serving as Campus Pastor for Redemption Columbia in Lexington, South Carolina under the leadership of Pastor Ron Carpenter, Jr. He is an Adjunct Professor for Lee University's Division of Adult Learning. He has served as a church planter, associate pastor, and youth pastor. He and his wife, LaShea, have traveled to more than 25 countries sharing the message of Christ. He and his wife have been married 23 years and have four wonderful children, Kiera, Makena, Aliyah, and Tegan. He is passionate about helping people live life to the full!

Why You Don't Need a Big Following to Become an Author

By Kary Oberbrunner

To find out more information about joining Author Academy Elite:

www.tinyurl.com/EliteAuthor

AUTHOR ACADEMY elite

REALIZE YOUR FULL POTENTIAL
STRESSRX.COM

WITH THE POWER OF ADAPTOGENS

StressRX™ is a unique blend of herbs that can provide the following benefits to your health:
- Strengthens the immune system
- Reduces the effects of stress
- Improves learning, memory, and reaction time

StressRX™ is the perfect supplement to add to your daily routine for a balanced lifestyle.

USE PROMO CODE **TCBOOK** FOR FREE SHIPPING ON YOUR FIRST ORDER.

Join us for a
Healing The Heart Retreat!

- A Healing the Heart retreat is truly a life changing experience.
- Healing the heart breaks you free from the pain of the past.
- When your heart is healed you will respond instead of react.
- Responding from a healed heart gives you the ability to heal your family.
- Healing the heart repositions you to experience life in a new way.
- Pastors Lee and Denise Boggs have led thousands of people just like you to a life of wholeness.

Schedule Your Retreat Today
www.livingwatersministry.com

Check out our other ministry opportunities:

Esther Retreat, Marriage Retreat, Pastors Only Retreat, and more!

Living Waters
MINISTRY